The *Vujá Dé* Diet Plan

Learn The Hidden Secrets On How To Break Through The Weight Management Battles

Ruby Fleurcius

The Vujá Dé
Diet Plan

Learn The Hidden Secrets On How To Develop A
Healthier Lifestyle From The Inside Out

Ruby Fleurcius
581 N. Park Ave. Ste. #725
Apopka, FL 32704
321-312-0744

Published in the United States of America
ISBN: 978-0-9990900-6-0
$14.95

Table of Contents

Dedication

I dedicate this book to my Lord and Savior who has so dearly blessed me beyond all measure. May this book break the strongholds of obesity. I would also like to take a moment to thank all of those who denied me love because of my size, saying that the love that I possessed from within my heart was not good enough. I would like to thank everyone who abandoned me when I was sick, struggling for my life, not knowing if I would wake up to see the next day. I thank all of my friends and family members for not checking on me to see how I was doing. From the depth of my heart, I really thank you for not bringing me one meal, I thank you for not taking me to one Doctor's Appointment, and I thank you for wanting me to secretly Die. I thank every so-called friend that laughed and talked about me putting on weight, as well as those who ridiculed me regarding their perception of my fall from grace. Better yet, I thank them for the way I was mistreated and how I was placed last, as if I did not exist.

It was in those toughest moments that I had to forgive, keep a smile on my face, and WILL myself to live, vowing to help others to do the same as well. It has taken all of that for me to release this book, "The Vujá Dé Diet Plan" out of the depths of my soul. Seeing all of that unfold before my very eyes, I could not leave this earth without leaving a legacy of information to heal the weary souls regarding this very issue. To be insulted by Doctors, friends, family members, etc. about my body, there was no possible way that God could allow me to endure such atrocities from those who have never invested in their bodies as I have. I had to find the reason, get it in writing, and create a Win-Win situation out of it all. And, being Ruby Fleurcius, I had to do something about it, I am Certified in Fitness and Nutrition, and for my health to spiral out of control was not a normal situation for me. I thank God that He allowed those individuals to bring this book out of me, so that I can empower the World with "The Vujá Dé Diet Plan" which is truly the Bread of Life for those who partake of it.

INTRODUCTION

Losing our self-image is one of the worst feelings that you could ever experience. This book reveals the secrets of how to deal with mental, physical, spiritual, emotional, and mental woes to ensure that you get exactly what you want, need, and deserve out of **The Vujá Dé Diet Plan**.

Applying Biblical Principles is the best way to gain control over our lives, and to learn the difference between being healthy and being overweight. If the truth be told, we will always find ourselves talking about living a healthy lifestyle, but why do we often make it such a hard task when it's just a choice away, or better yet, one prayer away? Well, **The Vujá Dé Diet Plan** has the answers that we have been waiting for. Throughout my journey through life, I have found that there are 4 reasons why we are overweight, underweight, unhealthy, or sick. They are:

1. What we are eating

2. What's eating us
3. Malnutrition
4. Hormonal Imbalance

If we take a moment to reflect on our failed diet plans, we will find that it has been our perception of our ideal weight, and the lack of prayer that has caused the most problems. I know about this all too well, and it's my reasonable service to share **The Vujá Dé Diet Plan** with those who are looking to lose the weight once and for all.

This plan is designed to open your mind to the people, places, and things that are preventing you from achieving what you want and desire. In my opinion, it is not about a fancy title, fancy car, big house, or luxurious office; it is about you achieving your ultimate purpose in life by changing the way in which you **THINK!**

In order to master the plan of your life, you must take your time to digest, study, and understand the information that pertains to you, what you are feeling, and the reasons why. It's imperative to allow this information to sink in, to prevent any form of overload; therefore, increasing your ability to turn your life around. There are no right or wrong answers; this is basically design to build the foundation of your awareness and your ability to become honest with yourself. Do not skip any section; they are all designed to work together to get you ready to embrace your destiny from within, building an attitude of substance that will withstand the wiles of life. Whether you share your information is totally up to you; however, the ultimate goal is completion. In this program, I want you to be totally honest with yourself; and frankly, your honesty may not include divulging personal or private matters with other people. If keeping your answers private ensures that your responses are absolutely honest, then please do so. Remember that this program is just for you, and it's your responsibility to release the true greatness that is already within you to get your body back to TEMPOLIC status.

Most often, we think that it is too late for us to do something about our lives, but I must say that it is never too late—as long as we have life in our body, there is hope. There will always be a Trail of Breadcrumbs left behind guiding us; however, we have to want to become guided. The Bread of Life will never lead us in the wrong direction because as scripture says, "I am the Way, the Truth, and the Life." John 4:6. In my opinion, trusting God for Divine Guidance creates a win-win situation—I am living proof, or I would not be writing this book. If God can take a Country Girl like me, and train her with the information that I am teaching; that is real POWER! There is no other way to explain it, besides the fact that it is available to those who are willing to glean from it to create their own personal journey. Is there any other way? Of course, there will always be another way, there will be the long way, the short way, there will be the right way, and there will be the dead-end; regardless of how we get there, our destiny is set. We can waste time, we can fight it, we can play around with it, we can cause ourselves to redo life lessons that we should have gotten right in the first place, we can cause our lives to become a constant bed of déjà vu, we can try to fill that void with something, and we can try to run from life, but we cannot hide. We will have to face it one day, and that day has come—that day is NOW with **The Vujá Dé Diet Plan**. This plan is designed to help you change your perspective on life, change your perspective about your body, and change your perspective about who you are from the inside out.

How do you know if this program is for you? Place a check in the box that applies to you.

- ❑ Is it hard for you to admit when you make a mistake or when you are wrong?
- ❑ Is it hard for you to reach out to people you don't know?
- ❑ Are you always trying to please someone else and neglect yourself?
- ❑ Is it hard for you to accept a compliment from others without feeling uncomfortable?
- ❑ Is it hard for you to be yourself around others?
- ❑ Is it hard for you to admit to your faults & weaknesses?
- ❑ Are you critical of yourself or others?
- ❑ Is it hard for you to acknowledge strengths?
- ❑ Do you feel intimidated by someone else's achievements?

- ❑ Are you always comparing yourself with others?
- ❑ Do you have a hard time complimenting yourself or others?
- ❑ Do you find it difficult to express love for yourself or others openly?
- ❑ Do you deny all your emotions and feelings?
- ❑ Do you hate being alone?
- ❑ Do you lie about your possessions in order to please others?
- ❑ Is it hard for you to make decisions?
- ❑ Do you avoid positive people?

If you have checked any one of these items, please continue this program. The haphazard way of living has a way of keeping us questioning life, when life is here to provide the answers. What is life trying to tell you? Or, better yet, what is that little nudge inside of you saying? If you don't know or don't care, you will find that history will constantly repeat itself in your life. Unwise decisions have a way of causing us to spin our wheels getting nowhere; and living our lives without a guideline will cause us to become easily frustrated, confused, and lackadaisical. There are times when we don't have a clue about what we want, what we are doing, or the reasons why; therefore, we begin to settle for whatever, expecting life to give us something, or someone that provides a temporary comfort.

In order to better plan your day, you must know what it will consist of or at least have an idea. Living every day "just because" is totally unacceptable when you have the ability to govern most things that happen in your life and how it will affect you. When you find the answers to your purpose, you are better able to ignite the passion that you have hidden within you and develop a healthier lifestyle. What you will find is that truly successful people are doing this day in and day out, and so can you—simply start writing out your goals, action plans, and time frames.

The Vujá Dé Diet Plan is not just about planning what you are going to eat from day to day; it is about planning your life. Of course, no plan is 100% full proof or problem free; every plan will have its ups and downs, the key is to find your passion, map, or plan out your passion, use your passion, and to share your passion—then everything else will work itself out. The Universe is designed that way; we cannot become defeated before we get started in whatever it is we have from within. Although our lives are full of change, we will all have different goals, different desires, different passions, different aspirations, different likes/dislikes; we just have a different everything—we are all uniquely created for a reason. Whatever that reason may be, we all have a purpose for being here, even if we are not ready to see it yet; however, it will remain invisible until we are ready.

Most often, we tend to think that we can attain true success and neglect other areas of our lives, such as our emotional, mental, spiritual, and physical well-being; and life will not have it that way. We must learn how to find balance in those areas of our lives; if not, we will overcompensate with something else as a crutch.

CHAPTER 1

GARDEN OF EDEN

What we put in our bodies say a lot about us, and vice versa. We as a people have become accustomed to taking the easy way out when it comes down to nurturing our bodies, and I would say nurturing our families as well. I firmly believe that we are indeed a product of our environment, and if we are not taught this information when we are young, then we are deprived of viable years of living a fulfilled lifestyle that could have been prevented through awareness. In all honesty, the pain that we are feeling regarding our bodies is of our own making.....everything that we do in life is a choice. We choose how we feel, and if we do not learn how to change how we feel about ourselves at our present size, we are not going to be happy with ourselves at any size, regardless of how small we become. It is all in the mindset. We must also know that we do not choose our body frame; however, we do have a choice to become and remain healthy.

In a world where heroes, champions, role-models, and idols are created, there are a vast amount of people who are really great, but do not realize it. Their mind, body, soul, and spirit are consumed with an itch that they haven't a clue on how to scratch; therefore, they find themselves filling in the blanks of their lives as they go along. However, what we need to realize is that this battle started in the Garden of Eden, when Adam and Eve partook of the forbidden fruit. We as descendants of Adam and Eve are still suffering from their actions. We have gone so far from the foods that were naturally intended for our bodies; such as God created foods opposed to man-made foods. The battle with food, the gluttony of food, the abuse of food, and the genetic manipulation of food are the primary cause of our obesity, and it will not stop until we understand how to bring our Mind, Body, Soul, and Spirit back under subjection of the Holy Spirit. In the next chapter, I will give you a better understanding of the Mind, Body, Soul, and Spirit; and, how it works together, but let me finish telling you what's really going on.

We have become divided by what we put in our bodies—there is no way around the truth in this matter. What we are eating will kill us in some way if we are not careful or if we do not become mindful of what we are consuming on a moment-by-moment basis. As we continue to make the wrong choices regarding what we are eating; or better yet, as we continue to partake of the forbidden fruit (unhealthy eating), we will continue to experience an inner itch of what's eating us. An itch from within is basically a longing that we all have, some more than others, but we all have a longing from within for something or someone. An inner itch can also be referred to as an inner struggle, spiritual warfare, vexed spirit, or a longing. The difference is that some people understand that they need help and that they need to work on themselves every single day, and some could care less about inner growth. However, with an itch that is not scratched or soothed, we will find that the itch becomes much stronger causing us to settle for people, places, and things that we are not happy with. Soon thereafter, the battle with obesity comes into play, as well as abusing our bodies with diets, or becoming consumed with our self-image to please others.

Life as we would call it, has a structural connection to everything and everyone that we hold dear to us. Our past creates an element of our present struggles from within, that controls our present and future actions, reactions, attitudes, and demeanor; therefore, determining the battle that we may endure with our weight that leads to some form of abuse. Although we have all suffered some form of known or unknown abuse; however, the ones with the biggest itch are usually the ones who are in the most denial.

A person with the feeling of unworthiness from within is most often depressed and/or stressed all the time. We will also find that their self-worth is so damaged that their self-esteem drops to an all-time low, subjecting them to abuse in many forms that are directly associated with an unhealthy lifestyle or the lack of the natural foods that help to combat stress within our bodies. Whether they are the abuser or the abusee, there are 10 main reasons why an individual abuse others or tolerate abuse:

1. Loneliness
2. Anger
3. Insecurity
4. Low Self-esteem
5. Conditioning
6. Helplessness
7. Broken heart
8. Obesity
9. Fear
10. Mental Disorder or Disability

The ultimate goal of an abuser is to seek power and precedence over something or someone. The love of power and the fear of losing it will drive an abuser to great extremes. Here are a few things that we need to know:

1. The pains of the past produce our problems with emotional eating disorders or extreme dieting.

2. The victim as a child often grows up to be victimized as an adult who has chronic self-esteem issues that use food for comfort, or starvation of the body for control.

3. Abuse victims often become a perfectionist and high achievers who abuse their body to fit into a certain clique.

4. Those who are abused, often become abusers who look down on others based on the food they eat or the size of their clothes.

5. Abuse victims feel they are to blame, so they blame others for their battles with their weight.

6. Headaches, asthma, body pains, and eating disorders are often symptoms of abuse or emotional problems.

7. Abusers are often respected people who disrespect others based on their image or size.

8. Angry people sometimes blame others for their misfortunes.

9. A negative self-image stems from real or perceived deprivation or rejection as well as abuse.

10. Sexual abuse often leads to sexual problems, promiscuity, or secret acts of prostitution and weight gain to cover up the pain.

11. Suppressed emotions often lead to physical symptoms that interrupt the hormonal balance in the body.

12. Forgiveness is essential for emotional healing to enable one to take charge of their health and make a commitment to living a healthy lifestyle.

Abuse is unacceptable, regardless of what type it is. Whether we are married, unmarried, obese, thin, or anything in between, when there is a battle from within, we will often ask ourselves:

1. What's wrong with me?
2. What have I done so wrong?
3. Why do I keep attracting these types of relationships?
4. Will I ever meet the right person?
5. Why am I so fat?
6. Why can't I keep the weight off?
7. Why am I so afraid to eat?
8. Why wasn't I born skinny?

Our conditioning or programming from our childhood experiences determine the level of anger we exhibit, our level of self-esteem, as well as our level of security. They amazingly work together regardless of whether we were raised by both parents, neglected by a parent, mistreated by a parent, lost a parent during childhood, abandoned, or whether we had surrogate parents, or raised by an institution—positive and negative programming will take place. For the individuals whose parents were physically or emotionally absent, rest assured that there will be self-esteem issues of unworthiness, unlovability, or insecurity that needs to be worked on or worked at on a consistent basis. When dealing with these types of issues, we very well may spend years unlearning, relearning, or getting over some things, but we must truly understand the point of origin if we want to really understand who we are as a person, and why we are as an individual.

I have found that negative experiences and hurt produces baggage; and, with every piece of baggage, the itch gets stronger and more frequent, while we pack on the pounds. Therefore, we must find a way to refuse the baggage that we do not want to keep, and the best way that I have found is through **The Vujá Dé Diet Plan**.

You are the best positive you that you have, so make the most of it. Of course, I know that you hear about this positive hoopla all the time; and I write as if it's so easy. I know personally that it's not always easy; especially when you are going through something. However, you must **TRY** as you surrender your body as a living sacrifice to God, therefore allowing your body to become the Temple of God.

CHAPTER 2

OUR TRUTH

As we continue to breathe the breath of life, emotions will flow through our veins whether we like it or not. Our emotions are a vital part of our being that we try to block out. And, it is through the blocking of our emotions that cause us the greatest pain, losses in life, and the most amount of weight gain. In order to truly embrace the essence of blissful living, we must understand and respect our emotions; if not, we will find ourselves emotionally bound on a diet roller coaster. If we take a moment to look around us, we will find that everyone is trying to knowingly or unknowingly fill a void from within—we are created that way.

A void that's ignored will cause the best of us to start looking for love in all the wrong places, going overboard to please others or simply trying too hard to make someone love us. Although everyone will have his or her own set of issues to deal with; however, when we have the facts about why we are doing what we do, we are better able to find the solution.

1 Corinthians 6:19-20 clearly states: *"Or do you not know that your body is the temple of the Holy Spirit who is in you, whom you have from God, and you are not your own? For you were bought at a price; therefore glorify God in your body and in your spirit, which are God's."* How is it that we have our blessings at our fingertips and become so blind to its power—when all we have to do is learn how to love ourselves enough to embrace all that life has in store for us. We are so blessed and don't realize it. Every day that we wake up, we are blessed to see another day; therefore, we must not allow the past to cloud our judgment and our desire to live a fulfilled lifestyle.

Most often, the things that are important to us do not include the things that are vital to our well-being. You will find that material gain is very important to people, and they are entitled to feel that way; however, let's talk about finding the importance in the real you. Now, in order to understand the real you, you must understand that God has given you everything that you need. He has given you a soul to live, a mind to think, a body to function, a spirit to worship Him, faith to know Him, the Holy Spirit to teach you, and His Word to live by. If you have a hard time understanding what I just said, let me break it down for you. You are a living soul with a spirit that dwells within a body, which happens to be blessed with a mind. Now, with that being said, it's imperative that you understand the difference between all 4 aspects of you.

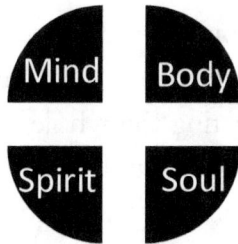

The mind is the instrument used for the output of what's stored in the brain and the soul, producing your thoughts on a conscious or unconscious level. Although the mind is essential in your day-to-day activities, it is a vital aspect of your brain that cannot be seen or touched. Without the mind, you would only be able to input information, but not receive the output. It is through the mind that you receive the ability to think, learn, understand, compare, comprehend, research, analyze, choose, create, observe, plan, reflect, remember, and reason.

When exercising these abilities, your manifested thoughts will contribute to your intellectual power, enabling you to experience the knowledge of your likes and dislikes; such as the expression of love or hate, happiness or sadness, desire or disgust, patience or anger, generosity or selfishness, as well as virtue or envy. Let's not overlook the fact that fantasy, romance, visualization, and role-playing takes place in the mind, often referred to as your imagination. This is a process in which your mind creates positive or negative images of the desires, goals, failures, and achievements.

Your mind is to your soul as your finger is to your hand. They are connected but have different functions that work together creating the whole unit. For example, if you broke your finger, would you put a cast on your whole hand? No, your physician would stabilize your finger, but the pain would be felt throughout your whole hand and possibly throughout your whole body. Better yet, if you remove every finger from your hand, you would still have a hand, but it would not function properly. So, if your mind is in turmoil, it will begin to permeate throughout your life creating dysfunction within the depths of your soul.

Mental management means managing time with your mind and the ability to exercise control over your thoughts. The only person that can destroy you is YOU! Your mind is like a bank account; what you put in it is what you can take out of it. No more or no less. Yes, you can accrue interest after thirty days, and whatever you deposit into your mind or whatever you think about for thirty days will accrue interest that is deposited into the soul, positively or negatively. Now, let me ask you, "How are you spending your time with your mind?" The way you think today determines what tomorrow holds for you and it will also determine how you feel and treat your body as well.

When people live life in the physical, the term used for the body is then called flesh, as opposed to living a spirit-led life and calling your body a temple. The body is not the real you! It is your means of coming into contact with the material or physical world, and it is also the visible entity that houses the invisible entities of your mind, soul, and spirit.

Take notice that you have two of every part of the body, except for the ones that are commonly misused. For example, you have one body that is prone to promiscuity, abuse, and laziness which equates to giving into fleshly desires; one mind that can be easily plagued with negative thinking and destructive thoughts; one nose that finds it more appealing to know everyone's business; one mouth that's inclined to gossip and belittle others; one tongue that is apt to cutting wounds into the heart of the innocent; one heart that becomes easily hardened and evil; one stomach that consumes too much or abuses food, alcohol, etc.; one head that is likely to become vain or arrogant; and one sex organ that is often misused before marriage and during marriage. What if you had two minds, two bodies, two noses, two mouths, two tongues, two hearts, two stomachs, two heads, or two sex organs? In my opinion, that would be devastating to mankind. I must admit that God had a divine plan for His creation, and it is obvious that you are truly a MASTERPIECE.

Accepting yourself for who you are, does not mean that you are not supposed to take care of yourself. Your body is a TEMPLE, so you have to take care of it. Choose the type of hairstyle, makeup, or clothing that reflects your own personal style and uniqueness. Real attractiveness is not just on the outside; it also comes from within. **The Vujá Dé Diet Plan** advocates that you change the things that you can, accept the things you cannot change, and love everything about you without complaining. God has given you one body that will last you a lifetime, and whether you like it or not, it is imperative that you take care of it. For the most part, what God has blessed you with, believe it or not, people are paying money to have! Now, with that being said, let's move on to what you really possess from within.

The soul is the most vital aspect of the body. Though the soul is unseen; it is as real as the air you are breathing right now. You are not able to see the air, but it is real. The soul is to the body as the marrow is to the bone. The bone dwells on the outside and the marrow, the lifeline of the bone, dwells on the inside. No marrow, no bone. The body cannot exist without a soul, and the soul cannot exist without a body. It is the spirit that operates apart from the body.

The soul is the vital center of all your intellect, emotions, feelings, and beliefs that form your character. Often it is referred to as the heart, inner man, or inner child, among many other names. The heart I will be referring to in this Chapter will not be the heart that pumps blood to the body, but the innermost being, center, or core of a human being. I consider the soul to be the storehouse of your emotions, revealing your positive or negative feelings of happiness or sadness, affection or rejection, fear or courage, gentleness or harshness, love or hate, pleasure or pain, and desire or disgust. Your soul governs you, and it has direct control over your will as well as your intellect, your character, and your personality. The soul is the part of you that rebels against God out of the desire for control. The soul has the free will to choose what it wants to do, when it wants to do it, and how it wants to do it. This is achieved by linking up to the satellite dish of your mind—channeling your every thought, choice, decision, or idea into what appears to be reality to you.

Your soul hides the secrets of your spiritual being. Man's life on earth has become warfare, because the soul stands between two worlds: the spirit world, which is linked through the spirit, and the material world, which is linked through the body; therefore, causing us to battle with ourselves over self-image opposed to self-preservation. Nevertheless, the soul cannot have the spirit world and material world at the same time because "No one can serve two masters, for either he will hate the one and love the other, or else he will be loyal to the one and despise the other. You cannot serve God and Mammon," (Matthew 6:24, NKJV). I assumed for many years that the word mammon meant Satan, but that was so far from the truth. Mammon means material gain or riches; therefore, the scripture states that you will worship God the creator or material gain. However, once this battle is in high effect, the battle with your health will become a prime factor based on the CRUTCHES one use to fill that spiritual void from within.

The soul of a human is given life at the first birth, when born from the womb. This is considered the "milking" stages of your life, preparing you mentally, physically, and emotionally to face the world, but if your milk is contaminated during this stage of your life, then so are you. The way in which you were raised during your childhood is a direct revelation of who you are today. In so many words, the hidden person of the heart reveals your attitude, values, beliefs, desires, education, essence, and habits. This explains why the soul is often referred to as your inner child. What is planted within the soul will come out sooner or later, exposing the real you. No matter how many masks you put on or how many personalities you assume, your character cannot be fooled. The moment you are put under pressure, what is inside your soul will come out; therefore, you must come to a true understanding of who you are from the inside out and not from the outside in. As you continue this program, I will show you how your life will come together by knowing what you feel, why you feel, how you feel, where you feel, and when you feel through the nudging of your spirit-man.

The word spirit has always sparked my curiosity; I knew that it was something sensitive and misunderstood by many. I must admit, I was told a countless number of times that the soul and the spirit are one and the same, but throughout my years of research on this subject, I have found that to be so far from the truth.

What is your spirit? I am so glad you asked. Your spirit dwells within the innermost depths of your soul. It allows you to communicate with, comprehend, contact, and worship God. It is a supernatural source that cannot be seen or touched, but produces guidance and discernment from within. This is commonly referred to as the higher self. It allows you to extend yourself beyond the material world as well as the limits of your own mind—tapping into the true essence of divine wisdom, courage, love, and compassion for God, oneself, and others.

The day that Adam and Eve sinned in the garden, they died spiritually, passing spiritual death on through all generations until the end of time. We are all born incomplete, missing this vital link that requires us to be born again. We cannot be born again in the mind, the body, or the soul, only in spirit. It is through your spirituality that your sense of consciousness is developed, giving you the spiritual eyes to see things differently and spiritual ears to hear the Voice of God. The human spirit is not the same as the Holy Spirit. The Holy Spirit is the spirit Himself bearing witness with your spirit, and your spirit is the channel through which the Holy Spirit will flow. The Holy Spirit is the third person of the Holy Trinity, which also includes the Father and the Son. The Holy Spirit revives your spirit and fills you with the abundance of life, love, compassion, mercy, longsuffering, forgiveness, and eagerness. Adam lost the Spirit in the beginning, but Jesus brought back the Holy Spirit and released Him to us once again giving us the Bread of Life saying, "I am the bread of life: he that comes to me shall never hunger; and he that believes on me shall never thirst." John 6:35; and I am now introducing that way of life to you through **The Vujá Dé Diet Plan**. Nevertheless, it takes the acceptance of the Lamb of God, who had no sin or blemish, to activate your spirit. God leads, teaches, and regenerates through the Holy Spirit, and He will also accuse or excuse an individual whose life does not line up with His Will or His Way. But it is the Holy Spirit that gives you the power to do that which you cannot do in your own strength, while illuminating the power of change from the depths of your soul. It is extremely important that you master these 4 aspects of who you are, and you will then find that making the appropriate adjustments in your life will become a piece of cake; therefore, creating a lifestyle that's able to fight off the Mind Germs of your past, present, and future. Guaranteed!

CHAPTER 3

THE MIND GERM

The enemy from within is not 100% your fault. The mind germ has to take responsibility for that as well. We are not often told about the mind germ because it is one of the biggest secrets known to man. Why is it the biggest secret known to man? I will tell you why? It is the biggest money maker known to man! In my opinion, we are not able to truly fight any type of germ if we are not aware of it; therefore, my goal is to bring about awareness in this particular area to bring healing to the mind, body, soul, and spirit of those that are innocently lost. **The Vujá Dé Diet Plan** Nuggets of Wisdom are not designed to be taken lightly—they are in effect, they are real, and they are here to stay; but it does not mean that one has to become consumed by it.

A Mind Germ is basically mental manipulation that preys on the impulses and weaknesses of those who are unaware of an intentionally planted seed. A Mind Germ is designed to provoke a reaction, thought, or desire to positively or negatively cross-pollinate its desired intent. Mind Germs are spread via advertisement, Television, Radio, Social Media, Emails, Newspapers, Cellphones, Text Messages, by Word of Mouth, etc. I am not saying that it is always a bad thing, but when it is mentally affecting our health, the way we are eating, the way we are taking care of our bodies, the way we perceive ourselves, and the way we are raising our families—then I would say, we should reconsider controlling that germ and not allowing that germ to control us.

The effects of the Mind Germ are very subtle—it's like something hypnotic. In my opinion, it's more imagenotic—okay, I am creating words here. What I am referring to is hypnosis done with images and sounds without our consent; which creates a whole new ballgame for me. A violation of our will—according to Biblical Law, cannot be done without the consent of the individual that's being influenced. However, the trick is, if one is swayed enough to believe in a product, service, or person, it provides an open gateway for Mind Germs to enter. If we are fighting a war from within the depths of our soul and we are not confident in who we are, we become subjected to this form of Mind Control; therefore, BEWARE. **The Vujá Dé Diet Plan** is designed to bring about an awareness of when we need to place our mind, body, soul, or spirit on a diet, especially when there is a battle from within.

In spite of your desires to change someone or

something, never allow the battle to cause war within your soul. Fighting against yourself about someone or something will cause you to become defeated in many different areas of your life. The secret to change is allowing it to be FREE! Allowing someone or something the freedom to change at its own free will is better than forcing an unwanted change to cater to your wants, desires, or needs. Change may not occur overnight; however, it will occur when you least expect it. All you need to do is allow it to flow—if it does not flow, there is nothing you can do about it anyway. So, there is no need to stress-out and allow the frustrations of life to destroy your sanity.

The warring power struggles, are no more than your conscience telling you to give up your desire for power regarding something or someone, in order to gain strength. **The Vujá Dé Diet Plan** believes that you should never engage in a war if you are not strategic about it. Jumping into something without an action plan could be devastating to your well-being. As a matter of fact, a power struggle will only set you up for repetitive mistakes and disappointments. Mistakes and disappointments in life will make you a more meticulous problem solver; however, it means zilch, if you do not take the time to find out the underlying reason for the warring in your spirit. Yes, I agree that some things just happen; however, if you allow your conscience to become your guide—you will always find the lesson behind the happenings as long as you do not whine about it or allow the Mind Germs of your past, the Mind Germs of your insecurities, the Mind Germs of your fears, or the Mind Germs of unforgiveness to prevent you from learning the lessons of life and moving on.

When there is inner turmoil, we strike out at other people oppose to striking out against ourselves. Not because we want to, we do it because it is easier to pass the blame. It is easier not to assume responsibility. Now, my question to you is, "Who is your enemy?" Is it Satan? No, it is not! Satan may use people, places, and things to get to you, but he is not your enemy in this game. The key to winning is assuming responsibility for your own role in your life. This may seem hard to swallow; however, the truth must be revealed, the real enemy is inside of you—the (inner me) enemy. For that reason, this is not the time to become closed-minded!

Ultimate success is always within your reach as long as you never give up on yourself during the stretch. It's easier to enjoy your successes when you are on top of the world, but what do you do when the world is on top of you? Do you cry, do you become depressed, do you become angry, do you blame others, do you eat your so-called pain away, do you try to drink alcohol to block out the issues of life, or do you give up? It is perfectly natural to experience one or all of these emotions when the weight of the world is on your shoulders.

However, what's going to make the difference is whether you give up or how long it takes for you to come out of that stupor. I, personally, consider the stretching process to be an opportunity for you to push beyond your self-imposed limitations.

The best way to bounce back from a Mind Germ is to remain calm and allow things to bounce off of you. The essence of your strength will reside in your ability to bounce back. No, it may not be easy to swallow your pride when life has embarrassed you. However, it is YOU that have the most power over your thoughts, words, and actions—so, if for some reason you fall, you have a choice to bounce back or break like glass. Bouncing back will give you the opportunity to excel and stand out. When all else fails, learn to overcome and abound even if you are on the rebound, while using the power that you have from within to bounce back and create the life you want. As a matter of fact, it is through a relationship with God that we will gain the courage, hope, faith, and peace to know and accept the REAL person from within.

Chaos is all around us. What can we do about it? Absolutely nothing, right? Wrong. The key to overcoming the chaos is to understand it. Although, some like chaos, some run from it, and some are condition to tolerate it; however, we do not have to become a victim of it. Change comes when we make the necessary sacrifices to put dead or chaotic things behind us. What's in the past is in the past! There is no need to bury ourselves in the things of old. Actually, it is the things of old that keep our heads buried in the sand of mental anguish. Furthermore, when we allow ourselves to become too mentally entangled in someone or something, rest assured that emotional bondage will soon follow like a thief in the night. Yes, most often it will take more than we are willing to give. Our willingness to put away dead things gives us the power to cope, the power to forgive, and the power to eliminate our sensitivities of being misunderstood. Every day in conjunction with the use of **The Vujá Dé Diet Plan** provides us with an opportunity to live better than we did the day before. Furthermore, when we allow ourselves to live in victory, we can begin to successfully lose weight allowing us to succeed in places that we never knew existed.

Putting things behind you will definitely give you a boost of confidence to move forward, when others are looking at the impossibilities at hand. God can and will do exceedingly and abundantly above all that you can ask or think as long as you trust, forgive, and believe that He can and will. Now with the emotional and mental issues out of the way, we are able to move on to the other factors of what's literally eating you.

Often we are taught not to love ourselves, but loving who we are as a person is vital to the success of our weight loss goal. The Bible speaks about being able to love your neighbors as you love yourself. So, that means that you are only able to love someone to the extent of how much you love yourself. I have heard some women say, "I love this man more than I love myself." I have a hard time believing that, because if you feel as if you love someone more than you love yourself—it is "INFATUATION." It is the in**FAT**uation that makes us FAT when the person we think we love fails to love us back. Trust me—that is the time we will eat ourselves to sleep; and, we cannot afford to take ourselves there mentally or emotionally—we need to love ourselves enough to put love in its proper perspective: love God first, love self, and then love others.

Self-love is one of the keys to putting our past behind us to embrace the true greatness of a healthy lifestyle. To say the least, a truly healthy lifestyle will not show up, if we hate ourselves—the overindulging, starving, and the yo-yoing will show up instead. We must learn how to love the good, the bad and the ugly secrets that we hold inside, while taking care of ourselves as we should. Self-love is not being conceited or selfish; it's about transforming our lives into something beautiful to benefit ourselves, and the lives of others. On the other hand, self-hatred deprives us of the opportunity to become a living testimony of love, grace, fulfillment, and pure health. The way we love ourselves will determine how others treat us; actually, we tell others how to treat us by our attitude, actions, and reactions. For example, if a man wants to be treated like a man, but his actions are childlike in nature—more than likely, he's going to be treated like a boy instead of a man. We set the tone for the way we are treated, so pay attention to the small things to ensure that the love that we have for ourselves is spread abroad to positively change lives.

When we compare ourselves with other people, we must question the love that we possess from within. Self-love allows us to accept our imperfections, understanding that God has made us unique in our very own special way. Besides, it's not a matter of being egocentric, conceited, or selfish; it's a matter of loving the skin we are in. Furthermore, if we can't love that about ourselves, it will be extremely hard to love that about someone else once the newness wears off. And, when it comes down to our emotions, love and fear are the stimulating factors that will build or breakdown our relationships. So, falling in love with ourselves and becoming a Temple of health is not a bad idea, because it will make our seemingly imperfections become our small blessings. If you are having a problem loving yourself or losing weight:

1. Make a list of positive affirmations and read them every day.
2. List 10 things that you like about yourself and read it every day.
3. Make your self-talk positive. If you say or think something negative about yourself, you must repeat a positive affirmation 10 times.

4. If someone says something negative about you, you respond back with something positive about yourself.

5. If someone gives you a compliment, say "thank-you."

Just remember, God broke the mold when He created us, so there is greatness in what He created. There is no need to fear it or idolize it, just learn how to embrace it.

CHAPTER 4

DIET IDOLATRY

Our diets are becoming our idol; we eat, think, and breathe diet after diet only to gain the weight back, and then some. I guess one would say, who am I to talk, I am writing a diet book myself..........absolutely! I have walked this road many times, and I am justified in writing this book. We are in this together, we must remain aware, and that is why I share my story.

I used food like a drug; I had to have it. I did not eat because I was hungry or needed nourishment, I ate because it gave me an escape from the real world. It temporarily changed my moods and pacified my emotions. If I did not eat what I wanted, when I wanted, how I wanted, I would get a serious attitude. Food began to control my life; my every thought was about food, the next new restaurant, etc. I was addicted to

FOOD, and I did not realize it! My siblings would often hurt my feelings by calling me fat, my friends would often pick on me about being chubby, my aunts would put me on the scale and compare my weight to theirs, and I was not even asked to my high school prom because I was too fat. Did it stop me from eating? Absolutely not, I was out of control, I loved food, I loved snacks, I loved sugar, I loved soda, and I knew nothing about a diet. I grew up in the country where everything was fried, real greasy, with some sort of pork added to it!

The best that I could do for myself was to pretend that it did not matter by using this statement, "More bounce to the ounce and more cushion for the pushin." Never letting anyone know that I would eat myself to sleep at night hoping that the pain would go away. The only time I did not feel the pain of life was when I would eat, and then go to sleep. I became very lazy, my only goal in life was to buy food, eat, and sleep. This was my true escape from my emotions; at that time as an inexperienced young adult, I knew no other way of making the pain of life go away.

Food became my best friend, when I wanted to express myself, I ate. When I wanted to go somewhere, I would go eat. When I wanted company, I would invite someone to eat. I felt that food gave me all the attention that I needed, or it could get what I wanted. Food never failed me until I found myself tipping the scale at almost

200 pounds. Needless to say, then food became my worst enemy!

I started with the dieting, and yes, I lost some weight, but the battles became my worst nightmare. I became paranoid about becoming fat even though I still felt fat at a size 6. After wanting to keep that size, I began to yo-yo from bingeing and purging out of control. Not only did I have my emotional issues, but I also had physical issues, and mental issues as well. I did not know what to do, so I began to wallow in my own misery with comparing myself with others out of jealousy, criticizing myself out of guilt, and gossiping about others out of arrogance, I just hated me, and I wanted to make everyone around me feel the same way about their bodies.

I was totally out of balance. Does being addicted to food make me any better than a person addicted to drugs, alcohol, cigarettes, relationships, or sex? My answer is no. I have found that being addicted to anything is bad for you, especially if it starts to consume your life. So, be careful when you look down on someone who's addicted to something, because you might be addicted to another thing.

Throughout my trials with food addiction and food deprivation, I have learned how to eat to take care of my body and to accept responsibility for my own actions and reactions toward food and my body. Most of all, the greatest reward has been the ability to open up my life to share my experiences to help others. In my opinion, diet tells you exactly what it means, Die represents (death from within), and the (t) represents the cross. "Dying" from the inside out, due to deprivation and starvation to become someone or something that you are not designed to become; therefore, it will take the cross, in the end, to save you because you will never be satisfied until you do it the right way!

What is the right way? The right way is the balance way as I stated earlier in the book—the approach mentally, physically, emotionally, and spiritually. God is indeed the secret ingredient to a healthy lifestyle. He is in control over all things, because He is the Creator; and, it is through Him, you will learn how to become discipline enough to keep the impurities in your body to a minimum. In becoming discipline, you will need a strong foundation (BALANCE) in order to approach your goals in losing those unwanted pounds.

As a matter of fact, I am tired of coming across these weight-loss schemes or pills that tell you how to lose weight, but not how to keep it off. The only positive aspects of those plans are quick weight loss, and the compliments you get. On the other hand, that same diet scheme will ruin your body, your esteem, and your self-worth when the weight comes back. The torture you place on your body with those quick-fix weight-loss diets, ruin your metabolism and make your body become your worst enemy. Yes, taking the weight off may be a breeze at times, but keeping it off may be a problem. The majority of people who lose weight regain it later. Most diets fail because of the lack of planning, long-term motivation, lack of pleasure, as well as deprivation and emotional turmoil. There is a better way of maintaining your weight without starving, bingeing, or purging. This is done by allowing the power of the Holy Spirit to bring your mind, body, soul, and spirit together into a healthy lifestyle. This will not happen overnight—it takes a little time to find out what is going on from within, as well as some spiritual soul-searching on your part that will be discussed later in the following chapters.

When we are out of control in regards to our eating habits, we tend to be out of control in our lives as well. Fear, anger, frustration, loneliness, shame, and jealousy could be the leading cause of overeating, poor eating, or compulsive eating; but, God is able to overcome all of those obstacles. We have been making excuses for the yo-yo dieting for years, and now it is time to put a stop to it. Yo-yo dieting is destroying not only our bodies but also our esteem as well. The individuals who are overweight or only mildly obese should avoid dieting alone, since strict dieting may worsen binge eating, lower metabolism, increase fat storage, cause muscle loss, cause irritability, and make dieters feel that they are starving and deprived if the underlying issues are not resolved effectively. When they are taking their bodies through these types of changes, they will develop a sense of guilt, failure, depression, hate for their body, and will possibly gain the weight back, plus more. However, it is beneficial to get involved in a weight-management program that helps to build esteem, self-worth, and body image. People who do not get into a weight-management program that teaches them how to deal with the inner-self may be setting themselves up for failure.

If you have not noticed by now, there are restaurants on every corner; not one, but several—the love of food is consuming our inner beings. We do not cook anymore. We depend on restaurants to do the cooking for our families; we depend on the restaurants to keep our families healthy because we do not have time to cook anymore; THIS IS AN EPIDEMIC. In my opinion, it's all a form of Mind Control as well—can one imagine trusting our health to someone we have never met? Can one imagine consuming food that we haven't a clue about what's in it? Yes, the food tastes good, but we cannot pronounce the ingredients on the label, or we haven't a clue about how long that item has been preserved before our consumption of it! Plus, we haven't a clue about how our food is being prepared, and the sanitary conditions of it. Food contamination is everywhere, and we must take responsibility not just for what's going in our bodies, but the sanitation factors of what we are consuming as well.

We need to make a commitment to God, allowing Him to control our desire to overeat or under eat, and allow us to get back into the kitchen and get our families healthy again. What I have found through my own journey is that prayer makes you more powerful, and the first step is to find out the real reasons why you eat or why you are not preparing healthy meals for yourself or your family. It may take a little bit of soul-searching on your behalf, because we are all creatures of habit! If you do anything long enough, it will become and feel normal. Just remember that food can't solve your problems; however, it may make you feel better for the moment, but the pain will return guaranteed!

Questions to ask yourself before you eat:

1. Is it pleasing to God?
2. Is it gluttony?
3. Will it nourish my body?
4. Will it edify my mind?
5. Will it make me stronger?

Make a personal assessment for yourself, because you know better than anyone else what you desire from your body. It is very important to know whether you want a lean body or an obese body, good health or bad health, good eating habits or bad eating habits, emotional eating or rational eating, etc. Becoming a slender, healthy person doesn't mean that you have to get rid of your favorite foods or spend all your time in the gym. Depriving yourself of all the things you like to eat will lead to bingeing or purging, and if you work out too much, you will get burned out. For these reasons, it is beneficial for you to learn how to use the three P's of **The Vujá Dé Diet Plan**: Pray, Plan, and Push Away.

PRAY for obedience in regards to your eating habits, so that you can continue to change your attitude about food and to exercise properly.   Most of all, give thanks because "he who eats, eats to the Lord, for he gives God thanks; and he who does not eat, to the Lord he does not eat, and gives God thanks," (Romans 14:6b, NKJV).

PLAN your meals, so you become more disciplined and committed to the upkeep of your body.

PUSH AWAY from the table before you overeat.   "So, whether you eat or drink, or whatever you do, do all to the glory of God,"

The body was not formed by God to be misused in any way, shape, or form, because our bodies are the Temples of Christ. If you make a mistake and overeat, pray about it, and understand that God is in control of your appetite, then move on. Lastly, make sure that you keep your body detoxified to prevent food poisoning from the hidden chemicals in our food.

CHAPTER 5

DETOX

The most significant part of **The Vujá Dé Diet Plan** is the Detoxification phase. Where there's a longing, we must take into account the seeds that we have planted over the years. When we take into account what we are giving, then we are better able to understand what we are receiving. Everything and I mean everything we do, say, think, eat, and drink becomes a SEED! And, it is up to us to determine whether or not our seeds will become positively or negatively planted, discarded, or held on to. The best way for me to explain this is to take you to the Book of Exodus in the Bible, where we have the Children of Israel on a Journey through the desert.

When the Children of Israel came out of Egypt, God provided a guide to them automatically, a cloud by day and a pillar of fire by night. Of course, it was taken for granted. Now, the guide (the Holy Spirit) will not be given to us automatically; we have to accept Him into our lives. Most people believe that there is a Holy Spirit, but negates the fact that the Holy Spirit is the most important factor and the divine connection to their successful weight loss.

Weight loss is not just about losing the weight; it's really about losing the inner pain that keeps you fat. If you would dare to trust the Holy Spirit with your eating habits or emotional rollercoasters, He will provide you with Direction (He will lead the way), purpose (He will illuminate the purpose that He has for your life), Provision (He will provide for the vision) and He will help you pray for things or issues that are unknown to you. Now, with that being said, here is the story:

As the Children of Israel journeyed through the desert, they became hungry. As usual, they complained to Moses about it—it behooves me that they were willing to go back into bondage and slavery just to fill their stomachs with fish, leeks, onions, garlic, melons and cucumbers for free. They did not realize that it wasn't really for free! However, Moses prayed to God, despite their vicious complaints, and God rained bread from heaven, which is commonly known as Manna.

God also gave them many different ways to prepare the manna, and the Children of Israel were still not satisfied—they wanted more. They wanted meat, if God intended for them to live off of meat, He would have rained down meat instead of manna or meat in conjunction with the manna. In fact, having meat was never God's original plan for them. God's first plan was THE PROMISED LAND with MILK AND HONEY! His second plan was to feed them bread from heaven. He was trying to deal with their slave mentality, and they were focused on their next meal, opposed to their next step. They spoke of freedom and continually thought about slavery—this is definitely an indication that the price of bricks and mud were more valuable to them than the freedom to create a life of whatever they wanted.

After the Children of Israel constantly complained to Moses about meat, God gave them meat to feed their fleshly cravings. He did not give them meat for one day as He does with the daily ration of manna—He gave them meat for a whole month. While giving into the murmurs and the lust of their flesh, they overindulged by partaking too much of something that they were not supposed to have anyway. By this one act of greed, eating too much meat caused a parasitic plague that took the lives of many. Due to the fact that they were not carnivores, their bodies were not able to fight off the infections and viruses; therefore, a lot of people lost their lives as a result. However, this provides us with an opportunity to go right, where they went wrong. Although this happened in the Bible, this is still happening right now in today's time, but with a slightly different up-to-date twist. We are still overindulging on food, our bodies are still not able to fight off infections, we are still getting infections from animals, we are still dealing with infestations, etc.

The wilderness experience is designed to purge you from the desires of wanting or giving in to your fleshly desires. GOD HEARS ALL MURMURS and now is not the time to murmur about what you don't have, what you can or cannot eat, or how fat you are—this is a time of soul-searching to understand the deeper meaning of the Manna that's presented in your life. What was "Manna" in the Old Testament is now your "Daily Bread" in the New Testament. Going through this phase, you will definitely have to walk by faith, and not by sight as you allow this to become your Bread of Life. Jesus tells us about the value of our daily bread in the Sermon on the Mount saying, "Give us this day our daily bread," in Matthew 6:11 of the Lord's Prayer; however, it still goes overlooked, day in and day out! Our daily portion is a Breadcrumb, and if we gather up enough, is it not the Bread of Life? A big crumb or little crumb, it is a Breadcrumb—the only difference is how we view it!

Our Breadcrumb is indeed hidden in plain sight— when we overlook our Breadcrumbs, when we live our lives out of purpose, or when we live our lives in some sort of bondage, it creates a life that's full of limitations and excuses that hinder our ability to embrace our purpose or passion. This is where your faith will be developed, put to the test and polished so you cannot weigh your body down with food to make you feel sluggish. Food is designed to make you feel energized and refreshed. If it's making you feel sluggish, sleepy, or lethargic—you are eating the wrong foods for your body. When your body is rejecting the food, you will feel tired or sluggish—it is God's way of symbolically telling you to change what you are putting in your body.

However, with **The Vujá Dé Diet Plan**, you are required to cut back on eating meat; and your serving portion cannot be more than the size of the palm of your hand. If your hand is small, that means that God has designed your body as a small framed body, and the same applies to a medium, large, x-large body, and so on. Do not be ashamed of your frame—God created different frames for different purposes; however, if your frame is unhealthy, overweight, and abused for the frame God has blessed you with, you need to do something about it. I am personally a large framed woman, and I am 100% happy because I eat totally healthy, I take care of the Temple the God has blessed me with mentally, physically, emotionally, and spiritually. When I look in the mirror, I am truly happy with who is looking back at me because I allow my conscience to be my guide, and I walk in Divine Purpose.

Life has a way of granting us the conditions in which we subconsciously choose. When given a little time, the seeds that we plant can and will produce after its own kind, regardless of when, what, how, where, and why it's planted. What about the seeds that remain unplanted? Great question, "NO HARVEST!" There are some seeds that we need to plant, and there are some that we should not plant.

Your lifeline is in the seeds that you are planting in your body mentally, physically, emotionally, and spiritually. Don't think for a minute that you are able to supersede the laws of the land, "SEED, TIME, and HARVEST." If we are eating badly, with time the harvest will come; and for that reason, it is imperative that we detox our bodies frequently. If our body is full of toxins, it is definitely harder to lose weight, because our body will begin to fight us back. **The Vujá Dé Diet Plan** deals with 2 types of Toxins:

1. Toxins from Foods
2. Toxins from a Parasitic Infestation

Both types of toxins are bad for our bodies, and need to be dealt with appropriately, if not we will get sick, gain weight, or have hormonal imbalances that cause major health issues. How do we know if we have a parasitic infestation in our body that's causing problems? Let's start with stomach problem such as:

- Abdominal Pain
- Bloating
- Bloody Stool
- Burning In The Stomach
- Chronic Constipation
- Diarrhea
- Digestive Problems

- Excessive Early Bowel Movements
- Excessive Gas
- Explosive Bowel Movements
- Hemorrhoids
- Leaky Gut
- Mucus In The Stools
- Nausea

The toxins that are in our system overload and overwork the organs while attacking the central nervous system causing:

- Chronic Fatigue Syndrome
- Excessive Weakness
- Lethargy
- Low Energy

When tissue becomes inflamed from the toxins, the body's white blood cells increase to defend the body. This reaction causes skin rashes and food allergies to appear, as well as the following symptoms:

- Allergic Reactions To Food
- Allergies
- Brittle Hair
- Crawling Sensation Under The Skin
- Ulcers

- Dry Hair
- Dry Skin
- Hair Loss
- Hives
- Itchy Anus
- Itchy Nose
- Itchy Skin
- Lesions
- Rashes
- Sores
- Swelling
- Eczema

These little critters that lurk from within can and will contribute to our mental instability issues causing:

- Anxiety
- Depression
- Forgetfulness
- Mood Swings
- Nervousness
- Restlessness
- Slow Reflexes
- Unclear Thinking

When the body is at rest, the toxic invasion of parasites takes over the body causing:

- Bed Wetting
- Disturbed Sleep
- Drooling While Asleep
- Insomnia
- Seizures
- Sudden Jilts while sleeping
- Teeth Grinding

To say the least, they also cause appetite, malnutrition, and weight disorders such as:

- Constantly Feeling Hungry
- Inability to Gain Weight
- Lose Weight
- Loss of Appetite
- Obesity
- Weight Gain Even When Being Malnourished

However, these little rug rats can travel to almost all soft tissue, taking over the joints and muscles. Once that is done, they begin to cause cysts and inflammation build up, which gets commonly mistaken as arthritis and muscle pain. And when they pool together, they cause:

- Arthritic Pains
- Back Pain
- Fast Heartbeat
- Heart Pain
- Joint Pain
- Muscle Cramping
- Muscle Pain
- Numbness of the Hands and/or Feet
- Pain in the Navel
- Shoulder Pain

These bloodsuckers take all the good vitamins, including iron; therefore, causing one to become:

- Diabetic
- Severely Anemic

Not only that, they cause one to have a weakened immune system causing:

- Cysts & Fibroids
- Erectile Dysfunction
- Menstrual Problems
- PMS
- Prostate Problems
- Urinary Tract Infections

- Water Retention
- Yeast Infections

This parasitic moocher also causes:

- Bad Breath
- Body Odor
- Excessive Saliva
- Fever
- Peritonitis
- Poor Immune Response
- Respiratory Problems
- Unclear Vision

As we can see, parasites are contributing to most of our health issues, but are not diagnosed as such. As most of us don't want to talk about this issue; but, if our bodies are becoming more infected by these microscopic intruders, we must do something about it. Now, it's up to us to take charge of our health and not allow something that we cannot see, cause us to lose ourselves outwardly. Doctors are not going to tell us that parasites are a major cause of our diseases, weight gain, fatigue, brain fogs, vision problems, and much more—this will cut off their residual income. Or, better yet, they will not be able to overload us with habit forming prescriptions to keep us legally hooked on drugs. There is a reason why the Drug Stores are on every corner; however, this is not designed for one to ignore medical attention or to stop taking their prescription medication, this is designed to bring awareness to what's really taking place within **The Temple of the Holy Spirit**.

For this parasitic reason, **The Vujá Dé Detox** is a prerequisite before embarking upon this weight loss plan. In order to effectively maximize this program, order your Herbal Detox at www.RubyFleurcius.com. Furthermore, if we deworm our pets, why are we not deworming ourselves? The eggs are all around us, and that is why 73% of the population today is unawaringly infected. This is an epidemic that is directly linked to our obesity, sicknesses, and diseases because they are robbing our bodies of its nutrition.

Let me talk about nutrition for a minute—we are created a certain way. In the beginning of time, we were created from the dust according to Scripture, and God has designed the earth to take care of itself. Therefore, if we eat what we are supposed to eat, our bodies would take care of itself; but, in today's time—that is not the case. We have a lot of toxins, and processed foods to deal with; therefore, if we do not know what foods to eat, our bodies will not fight off these little critters, so they take over. They are doing their job, to find a host and to invade and take over—now, it your job to get an understanding to take care of your body to ensure that they do not take the essential vitamins and minerals that you need, in order to have a fulfilled life. I am not giving you this information to scare you; I am giving you this information to empower you. Germs and parasites have been around since the beginning of time, and they are not going anywhere. However, you need to become educated regarding what can happen to your TEMPLE if you do not take care of it! For example, if you leave a building unmaintained what will happen—weeds, creatures, mold, spiders, etc. will take over; that is how the Universe is created to bring that building back to the dust from which it was created.

We need nutrition; our bodies need the natural vitamins that are found in living fruits and vegetables. Although, we can use dietary supplements; however, we must eat our fruits and vegetables, because they have the natural enzymes that our bodies need that man has not even discovered as of yet. The manufactured fruit and vegetable drinks cannot replace the all-natural fruit, so don't be fooled by the hype. If you prefer to take a supplement, take it in addition to your fruits and vegetables; but, never as a replacement. Here are **The Vujá Dé Diet Plan** Signs of malnutrition:

- If you are losing your hair.
- If you bruise easily.
- If you have a hard time getting to sleep at night.
- If you are not eating a well-balanced meal.
- If you are very impatient.
- If you feel drowsy all day.

- If you always feel stressed.
- If you are nervous all the time.
- If you feel like you are very lethargic.
- If you feel as if you cannot find the willpower to do the simplest things around the house.
- If you feel as if your brain, eyes, or face is twitching.
- If you are feeling extremely constipated or you are pooping pellets.
- If you cannot lose weight or gaining an enormous amount of weight.
- If you have serious mood swings
- If you are easily upset by petty things.
- If you cannot control your anger.
- If you are having cramps in the middle of the night.
- If you are having lower back pain.
- If you are having excessive skin problems—too oily or too dry.
- If you have a problem digesting your food.
- If you have a problem passing gas.
- If you are having water retention.
- If your nails are dark, brittle, or peeling.
- If you are having a hard time concentrating.
- If you are constantly forgetting things.

- If you are feeling easily confused.

- If you feel as if your mind is going blank.

- If you are feeling tingling in your fingers or toes.

- If you are having a problem with depression.

- If you are having a problem with cracked lips or feet.

- If your nails refuse to grow.

- If you are having stomach problems, pain, or nausea.

Today, choose your seeds carefully, as you discard the negative seeds that are intentionally or unintentionally causing havoc in your body to ensure that you are ready for the Secrets of **The Vujá Dé Diet Plan**.

CHAPTER 6

THE SECRET

The most common emotional blocker is the fear that keeps us from truly cultivating our unique self. The surface issues that we experience from fear is by far created its own set of havoc in our lives. However, it's not too late. We have to understand the underlying root cause of why we fear whatever or whoever it is. Most often, when we are constantly hurt in relationships whether it is with a male or female, we start to build a wall of protection. The more we become hurt, the higher our walls become, and the more we close ourselves off to people, places, and things. Of course, this is our way of protecting ourselves; but, are we really protecting ourselves? The answer is no.

When we build walls or if our walls become so high, we don't allow the people, places, and things that we desire into our lives; therefore, we begin to use food as our comfort. Actually, we don't realize that we are causing our own anger, resentment, loneliness, weight gain, unhealthiness, etc. When we find ourselves dealing with walls, we will find ourselves dealing with the lack of trust. Most often, we think that having fear is a weakness, but it can be our greatest strength, if we allow ourselves the opportunity to learn through our fears, or to learn in spite of our fears. By doing so, wholeness and restoration will be waiting for us to reach out and claim. Rest assured, when we become tired of being unhealthy, overweight, or our issues get serious enough, fear will not stop us!

It is our faith that breaks all the barriers of fear that would cause our issues to overtake us. Fear drives us to use our faith to gain wholeness in an area that has broken us down for years. Here are a few things to ask yourself about fear:

1. What are you afraid of?
2. Why do you feel as if you are bound by this fear?
3. Do you know the root cause of this issue?
4. How do you feel when you experience this form of fear?
5. Are you willing to face this fear?

Persistence has a dynamic way of giving us the ability to supersede the lack of motivation; especially, when mediocrity is knocking at our door. The hand of our motivation has a way of reaching out to us when we take the initiative to do the legwork first. Listen to me well, even if we lack the motivation to do something about our lives, we can still achieve dynamic results through our ability to take action. Motivation will gradually lose its value if it's not applied—motivation without action means zilch, if we do not put some action behind it. Now, on the other hand, taking action without motivation can and will lead to many achievements on various levels. However, it will not enable us to become persistent; therefore, causing us to give up easily when the slightest form of resistance presents itself in our lives.

I know it's impossible to stay motivated 100% of the time, and I know it's also impossible to take action 100% of the time. Yet, it is through our motivation and our ability to take action that generates the persistence needed to keep us on track; therefore, creating Self-Discipline. As we all know, life has a way of causing us to work for what we want and to want what we work for. For that reason, we must understand that discipline is the key to persistence and persistence is the key to discipline. They are designed to work together, and when we leave one out, we will become confused or frustrated with our results or the lack thereof. It takes guts to keep moving forward when life is trying to push us in the opposite direction. However, if we can find a way to stay focused, we are better able to overcome any obstacle that could easily beset us and we are also able to determine the things that are absolutely not working in our lives. And, yes, taking action will sometimes require us to get rid of some unfruitful things or to make some adjustments in our lives.

Regardless of what you are faced with, never give up on you! Even if you feel like throwing in the towel on your weight loss, keep the faith, call on the help of the Holy Spirit, and keep moving forward in a positive direction. This will ensure that you are able to keep yourself moving until you are able to get your groove back. When you are super clear about what you want, life has a way of bringing the best out of you through adversity. Oh by the way, when you start seeing the results of your persistence and your self-discipline—you will get motivated real quick! So, don't wait to feel motivated, get a plan, plan your work, and work your plan. And, watch how the desires of your heart begin to bring you what you cannot buy, and that is the ability to motivate yourself. Everything that you need is already within you!

Loving the skin that you are in can motivate and encourage you to lose those extra pounds like nothing else can. At this stage of the game, you must learn how to manage your mind, or your mind will manage you through comparisons. A chattering mind without any applied wisdom will create a bed of doubt; therefore, causing you to rationalize and justify everything. Once this happens, the chattering will do its best to keep you in an imbalanced state of mind, dragging you down into a pit of turmoil and confusion.

The motto of Satan is, "kill the head, and the body will soon follow." When Satan plants a thought, your mind takes it and runs with it, whether it is the truth or pure speculation. Satan will try to hit you where you are the weakest. Actually, Satan knows that you cannot believe his lies unless you reject the truth first. He knows that what you have within you is more powerful than he; but, if he can deceive you and cause you to hate yourself—that puts the ball in his court. If not for anything else but that reason alone, stop comparing yourself with others, and let go of all the excuses for not appreciating the person that you are. Keep the chatter to a minimum. Bear in mind that you are in complete control over the thoughts you think and the actions you take on a moment-by-moment basis. So, if you want to be happy where you are going, it is essential to be happy where you are.

The Secret

Most often, your weight loss treasure is right under your nose! However, it's up to you whether or not you take the time or the opportunity to get rid of the junk and sift through the dirt to get to what rightfully belongs to you, and that is getting your body back.

Jesus awarded us the Holy Spirit when He ascended into heaven, even though we may not have been worthy of it at the time, but He awarded the wealth of the Holy Spirit anyway. Being healthy is your divine birthright, waiting for you to claim. It has nothing to do with your marketing strategies, tricks, or tactics—this is your "SECRET" for life. It's all about possessing what is already within YOU! How do you possess what's already within you? According to Matthew 17:21, "Some things only come out through fasting and praying." I have found fasting and praying to be a powerful SECRET that goes overlooked. When you awaken the Holy Spirit through fasting and praying—it will rout anything that you are going through. Fasting alone will not do it—fasting, praying, and invoking the Holy Spirit are the vital ingredients of a truly healthy lifestyle to keep the mind, body, soul, and spirit in top condition. There are many different types of fasts, but it is your responsibility to pray for the type of fast that's needed aside from the modified fast that is incorporated in **The Vujá Dé Diet Plan**.

Cleaning up the dust and debris in our lives will help us find peace from within, and it will also help keep the baggage of life from getting too heavy for us. Furthermore, we must find a way to appreciate everything we have and everything around us, the good, the bad, the right, and the wrong. As we very well know, life is full of surprises, and there is no reason for us to settle for a life of mediocrity when opportunity is knocking on our door through our ability to fast and pray.

Fasting is voluntarily humbling ourselves before God. This is accomplished by replacing a meal or several meals with prayer for a designated length of time. There are many different types of fasts:

1. A liquid fast, which allows only water or juice.
2. A fast consisting of only fruits and vegetables.
3. Refraining from eating meat only.
4. Eating one meal a day.
5. Sacrificing a meal a day.
6. Sacrificing Television.
7. Sacrificing extracurricular activities.
8. Sacrificing sexual relations.
9. Sacrificing any type of habit.

Fasting is to be used to receive the fullness, guidance, and power of the Holy Spirit flowing through you. Fasting is not to be used as a weapon to get money, houses, cars, or other worldly possessions. These things may come from the result of a fast, but fasting primarily for material gain is considered to be a fast for the wrong reason.

When we become caught up in the issues of life, we tend to let our guards down in hope of receiving attention to fill an unrecognizable void. And, when we fill that void with something other than what we are really missing, we will find ourselves trying to undo things that are already done, doing things that we should have left alone from the beginning, or attracting people, places, and things that are out of character for us. Furthermore, it's highly impossible to receive or attract the treasures of life if we have too much junk blocking our way.

13 Most Common Life Distractions

1. Overeating
2. Socializing too Much
3. Relationship drama or a Needy Relationship
4. Peer Pressure
5. Too Much Sleep or Too Little Sleep
6. Laziness or Slothfulness
7. Fear
8. Ego
9. Greed
10. Lack of Determination
11. Guilt
12. Loneliness
13. Depression

The positive or negative energy that is bound inside of you will eventually find a way to be released sooner or later. Your body will send you signals when you have an additional amount of positive or negative energy inside of you that need to be released. The signals may come as a headache, anxiety, backache, heartburn, fatigue, acne, loss of hair and things of that nature. However, when these signals are ignored, stress or depression is inevitable. Keep in mind, everyone's body is a little different—your goal is to find out how to release the trapped energy that's inside of you and when the Spirit of the Lord is leading you to go on a fast. Take some time out to listen to your body—not doing something positive will hurt you just as much as participating in something negative. Your body is an alarm system that helps you fine-tune your intuition. And, paying attention to your intuition will help relieve stress and help you release some of that creative energy that is inside of you. There is always a way out, and the answer lies within you. Your ability to deal with issues or problems will be your ticket to becoming free—free from false expectations. Your freedom is very important, especially when you want to soar to the top.

Let's talk about commitment for a minute—commitment is not meant to be comfortable nor convenient; it is meant to give you an opportunity to become a team player that's committed to winning. Commitment is basically placing your trust in a person, place, or thing; I have found that without trust, there is no real commitment. There will be some commitments that you will need to keep, and there will be some commitments that you will need to let go of. Trust me; it is very hard to stay committed to a lost cause. Furthermore, with a commitment comes responsibility—no matter what you do in life, you are solely responsible for your actions, reactions, and the lack thereof; therefore, if you need to fast to kick a habit—DO IT! If you need to fast to commit to the leading of the Holy Spirit—DO IT!

CHAPTER 7

KICK THE HABIT

In order to embrace **The Vujá Dé Diet Plan**, we need to pay attention to what's going on within us as well as around us. Our path of mastery is determined by our ability to reach beyond our self-imposed limitations to assume responsibility for our actions, reactions, and the lack thereof regarding our eating habits, and how we are taking care of our bodies.

Most often, it is easier to blame someone else or make excuses for our weight problem, but guess what? It doesn't solve anything. If we take a moment to look back over our lives, we will find that the issues that we are having right now, are the issues that we did not pray about, the issues that we did not seek God about, the issues that we did not fast about, or the issues that we did not exercise the wisdom that was available to us at that time. Therefore, shifting the blame has become easier, or better yet, emotionally comforting than to take responsibility for our actions, reactions, or the lack thereof. Now in order to kick any sort of habit in your life, it is going to take discipline, direction, and determination on your behalf.

Weaknesses are the hidden opportunities of mastered habits or routines. I have found that the center of a weakness is OPPORTUNITY! Most often, we look for opportunity in everything and everybody, while forgetting about the opportunity that comes from within. We all have room for improvement, and admitting a weakness is the first step to overcoming it, getting through it, or maximizing it. As a matter of fact, one of the best ways to master a weakness is to become a master over the habit(s) or routine(s) that contributed to the weakness in the first place. For example, if your weakness is getting up late, you can master it by getting up early every day, and the list goes on. There is no need to be ashamed of a weakness; however, there is a need to be ashamed of not working on a weakness. Getting creative with your weaknesses will help eliminate shortsightedness. Just remember, the creative force that's within you will propel you into your destiny regardless of what others think of your weaknesses or strengths.

Healing for the sore eyes of despair is wrapped in your willingness to keep a smile on your face, especially when life is not smiling back at you. Eyesores are designed to inhibit your vision, creating a wide variety of blisters that will block your innate ability to deal with or handle life. At times, life can and will get a little painful, but can you handle it? Or, better yet, let me ask you, "Can you handle things that are not going your way? Can you handle failure? Can you handle rejection? Can you handle being abandoned? Can you handle being ridiculed? Can you handle being frustrated? Can you handle being confused? Can you handle being betrayed? Can you handle lack?" These are the most common pitfalls that occur when you have a desire to have more than what you have right now. In order to sustain your vision, goal, or desire, life is going to require you to answer "yes" to each one of these questions. Your pain is really doing you a favor. Pain and disappointment will sometimes open your eyes to the truth about your strengths and weaknesses. As of today, your pain is your gain! Once you understand this, regardless of what size you are, it will enable you to keep a smile on your face when others have nothing to smile about.

If our past could speak, what would it say? If our present could speak, what would it say? If our future could speak, what would it say? These are some questions that we must ask ourselves when dealing with our weight loss battle or kicking our bad habits. We cannot be clueless, or careless about what we want, what we do, what we say, or what we become. We are held accountable for our actions, reactions, or the lack thereof when it comes down to our Spiritual Walk with God, and the prayers that are going to keep us on track. Although we do not talk about instincts much when we are talking about prayer; but, our instinct is our communication link in order to know what to pray for, when to pray, how to pray, where to pray, and why we need to pray. It is our instincts that wake us up in the middle of the night to pray, it is our instincts that let us know when something is wrong, it is our instincts that allow us to embrace Godly eating habits, it is our instincts that awaken the spirit from within, and it is our instincts that allow us to connect with the Holy Spirit.

Now getting down to the nitty-gritty, there are a few habits that we need to kick in order to succeed on this program:

1. No sodas, not even diet sodas or carbonated drinks.
2. Stay hydrated with water, minimum 8 cups a day
3. No artificial flavors
4. No processed meats, fresh meat only.
5. No packaged meals
6. Watch out for the hidden sugars
7. Only eat out of a saucer plate. If that's not possible, eat only half of your meal and save the rest for later.
8. Fresh or frozen fruits or vegetables only, no canned fruits or vegetables.
9. Choose your meal or the dessert when eating; you cannot have both in the same meal.
10. Limit television, food commercials will invoke food cravings

Adhering to **The Vujá Dé Diet Plan** is not about strict dietary confinements, staying unreasonably thin, or denying yourself of the foods you adore. It's about feeling awesome, having more vitality, enhancing your lifestyle, and balancing out your state of mind to learn how and what to eat at the appropriate times. **The Vujá Dé Diet Plan** ultimate goal is to help individuals to utilize straightforward weight loss tips that slice through the perplexities of losing weight and keeping it off. This is accomplished by offering solid eating routines that are as useful for your brain as it is for your body.

Limitations are created in the mind when there is codependency residing in the heart. This is not the time to become closed-minded! Everyone may not be going where you are going; they may not look the way you want them to look, and they may not have what you expect them to have. But, trust me, there is always something to learn from a person who maintains a focused and positive outlook on life. You should always remind yourself that you possess unlimited potential, regardless of the opinion(s) or judgment(s) of others. And when you do this, it enables you to become interdependent, allowing everyone to play his or her role in your life.

I am challenging you to earn your keep, releasing the true desires of your heart that provides liberation to you mentally, physically, emotionally, and spiritually. In the meantime, setting a guard over your thoughts is always the wisest thing to do when trying to kick any form of habit. This will ensure that you are able to mentally leap over obstacles that periodically catch you off guard. From my experiences in life, being caught off guard with an obstacle in your life, is not a great feeling; especially, when you had no clue that it was coming. In order to successfully overcome obstacles, you must think about what you are doing and what's going on around you. Focus and control are in your mind; it only takes a fraction of a second to gain or lose control. Therefore, having an open and guarded mind will help you deal with everything on a moment-by-moment basis. This will also ensure that you do not let any circumstance or situation linger in your mind longer than necessary. By doing so, it will help you deal with:

1. A Double Mind.
2. A One Track Mind.

In order to attract success, or attain a goal, you must have a stable mind, because according to James 1:8, "A double minded man is unstable in all his ways." If you have not noticed, confusion comes into our lives to prevent us from making up our mind, or to get us off track. Most often, we don't realize that we have to take control of our tendency to become double-minded; especially, when one part of us wants to go in one direction while the other part of us goes in the other direction. We are constantly bombarded with too much to do, too many places to go, too many people to see, too many calls to make, and too many unaccomplished goals.

No matter what happens in life, or what does not happen, you must always remain positive with an open mind to prevent self-sabotage from breaking your flow. Once again, never fall into the trap of Murphy's Law, it will hinder your creativity—things are made to go wrong, to go right and things are made to go right, to go wrong to keep you on your toes. That is just the cycle of LIFE. Frankly, your best option is to find a way to work around your limitations, taking nothing for granted.

The "your way or the Highway" mentality or the one-track mind is basically a mind that holds on to many secrets, fears, and doubts about life. As the battle rages in their mind, they are in such a state of denial that they really feel as if they are in control. Not only that, they tend to control everything around them to give the appearance of having everything together. This person is too self-sufficient to be teachable—so they prey on weak-minded individuals who allow them to dominate and control them. However, as a word of caution: PLAYING MIND GAMES WILL ONLY WORK FOR SO LONG.

The peace in your life starts with the ability to

become flexible; if not, you will put yourself in a position to become a stiff-neck. A stiff neck person is basically a person who is stubborn. It is amazing how stubbornness will cause an individual to refuse to face reality; therefore, causing them to become sidetracked by distractions that could have been easily avoided. Those who are too stubborn to become flexible, are usually the ones that break real easy. I must admit, things may not always go our way, but if we replace our stubbornness with flexible discipline—all things will work together for our good. With that in mind, take a moment to listen to what your heart is saying to you while your flexibility moves you into your rightful place with unlimited possibilities to allow the Mind of Christ to abide.

What's the purpose of Christ Mindfulness? The Mind of Christ is not self-centered. The Mind of Christ is SUBMISSIVE TO THE WILL OF GOD. The Mind of Christ is a rewarding mind. The Mind of Christ will help you kick any habit. And, when you allow the Mind of Christ to guide you—it will change your behavior, thoughts, desires, and attitude, giving you a peace of mind that supersedes all human understanding. Not only that, it will allow you to become open-minded, flexible, guarded, and committed to allowing the passion inside of you to come forth releasing all of those unwanted pounds that are not conducive to your body frame.

Thinking adjustments are designed to keep your mind free and clear of any unwanted cobwebs. Everyone will have some sort of fears and doubts in life—the difference is that some will choose to adjust their thinking process, and some will choose to bounce thoughts around in their mind; eventually, causing them to become confused, frustrated, and sometimes depressed. If you are feeling this way, it is time for you to do something about it. My friend, making adjustments in your thinking process will cause you to take responsibility. If you are not sure how to take responsibility for yourself, start writing it out and ask yourself fact-finding questions. You are the expert in your own life, simply because you have the ability to make minor adjustments—turning a negative situation or circumstance into something positive. The adjustments that you make today can and will have an effect on your ultimate destination. Trust me, with a slight attitude adjustment and humility, you can turn your insecurities and weaknesses into the epitome of great success.

CHAPTER 8

DIET OF HUMILITY

Our freedom will always cost us something; it may be uncomfortable, but there will be a sacrifice whether we like it or not; and I have found that our humility can break the chains of our past quicker than any form of arrogance, any day! The Children of Israel constantly spoke of freedom, but the chains, as well as the enslavement of their heart, kept them bound. There are times when we can't see ourselves as being free, and we would rather go back into an uncomfortable situation, rather than making the sacrifices necessary to secure our future.

Living a life of mediocrity will work for some; but for the most part, we are born with a desire to strive, succeed, and possess. However, when we get to a fork in the road, we tend to question life. A fork in the road is merely an illusion created within oneself, causing the mind to fight against what's in our heart and vice versa, especially when it comes down to eating healthy or eating what tastes really good. When we fight against our past eating habits, it breaks the communication between our heart and mind. Our heart and mind are like a river; they should flow together—if they are not flowing, or you feel as if you are going against the current, SOMETHING IS WRONG! Who knows—it may be stress, fear, anger, guilt, resentment, unforgiveness, or negativity blocking your flow. So, what do you do when your heart is telling you one thing, and your mind is telling you another? Great question, my friend! You need to find out what's blocking your flow and deal with it accordingly. If you are not sure about something in your life, start writing it out and free your mind. This is done by asking yourself fact-finding questions. As I said earlier, you are the expert in your own life, simply because all the answers to every problem, situation, or circumstance reside within you. Get into the habit of putting your thoughts in writing and reviewing them periodically—this will prevent undue battles between your heart and mind; therefore, breaking the cycle of mediocrity.

Break the Cycle
Gratefulness is a pool that you need to jump into from time-to-time to ensure that you keep a refreshed, positive outlook on life. There are times when you may

ask yourself, "What do I have to be grateful for?" And, this is a legitimate question to ask, especially when you are counting your blessings. Throughout my own personal experiences, I have found that counting your blessings is extremely helpful when you are feeling down about something or someone, or when you have a desire to overeat. Most often, we remember the negative things that happen to us, more than we remember the positive. It is amazing how we remember pain before pleasure when it should be the other way around. I have found that if you remember the pleasure before you allow yourself to feel the pain, it can and will remove the sting of undue stress and the tendency to abuse food, overeat, or under eat. Your best bet is to keep a list of your blessings and read them before you allow your emotions to take a dip in a pool of negativity. My friend, gratefulness and our ability to become humble are two of the hidden secrets on how to charm the heart of any person or open doors that were previously closed to you.

Bumps and Bruises

Turning your back on life will cause it to bump into you, with or without your approval. The bumps and bruises of life are not considered to be a joking matter. Life can hit you so hard until it knocks you flat on your face; however, falling flat on your face is not a bad thing as long as you get back up.

There are many different reasons why life knocks us around a little bit; but most often, the reason is DISOBEDIENCE! On occasion, we all walk in blind disobedience without realizing it, because we want what we want when we want it without evaluating the reason(s) why we want it, praying about it, or fasting over it. Of course, you will not be able to control everything that happens to you, but you can control how you deal with it. Spiritual discomfort comes to push you out of your nest of mediocrity. Your best bet will be to face life head-on; this will ensure that you are able to at least see what's coming at you. And, if you have not noticed already, life is a gift; it is imperative that you accept it, embrace it, and never turn your back on it.

Most often, we look at mediocrity as a bad thing, and it only becomes a bad thing when you become stuck. Stuck in the past, stuck where you are, stuck in a rut, etc. As you know, life is full of surprises, and God will sometimes place you in a mediocre state to prepare you for a blessing, grow you through a blessing, or strengthen you for the next level of your blessing. However, if He places you there, you must understand it's only a temporary state, and you will not be there long. In order to rise above mediocrity, you are going to have to make a few sacrifices, and that means "WORK." Yes, you need to take action. Working diligently, in the spirit of excellence with your faith in hand, is the wise thing to do, especially when you are limited. What I have found is that limitations are designed to be temporary unless you opt to make them permanent; therefore, it is best to stay in the NOW! Yes, it is imperative to set goals for the future; but, it is really what you are doing right now that will prepare you for tomorrow. So, put the past behind you, set goals for tomorrow, and enjoy today. Trust me, life will become easier, and the pounds will begin to fall off.

Perception, perception, perception—we can't get away from it. When we walk, our perception is there. When we talk, our perception is there. When we think, our perception is there. When we take action, our perception is there. No matter what we do, our perception has a way of tracking us down. In order to survive in the real world, there are 3 things that we must possess, and that is respect, humility, and discipline. We will find that our unparalleled sacrifices are usually made in the areas in which we lack discipline or the areas that we lack respect.

Humility is the true sign of controllable strength. As a matter of fact, humility is the main ingredient that prevents you from becoming snobbish, rude, arrogant, selfish, inconsiderate, or disrespectful. In order to embrace a truly healthy lifestyle, a turn-around is required to embrace true greatness, while others talk, yearn, and waste time. Anything that we work on long enough with discipline, action, and commitment, in time we will become an expert at whatever it is, if our time is not wasted.

Wasting time is definitely listed on all of our resumes at some point in our lives. However, when we continue to squander precious time, we will find that we are at a loss for something that will eventually cause us to become codependent. My friend, regardless of whether we are codependent or interdependent, there is nothing better than having our own. Now, in order to have our own, we must become disciplined in our actions and reactions, whether that action is in prayer, fasting, working longer, harder or smarter, etc., discipline is a must! With that being said, anything or anybody that's worth having should be worth the sacrifice; if they are not, then we are definitely wasting our time. When we choose to move forward in greatness, we will; and, until we are ready, we will remain where we are, or where we have been. If we really want to know and understand the choices that we have made, simply evaluate our actions, reactions, and activities. Trust me, they will reveal our choices without anyone saying one word.

The denial of what's real can and will cause your reality to get out of control, giving your reality power over you. One of the worst feelings to experience is to have your reality make choices for you as you wallow in a painful pool of self-pity regarding your weight. Here's how to take charge of your weight loss in total humility:

1. Overlook the fad diets, they come and go – without offering a permanent solution.

2. Set realistic goals: **The Vujá Dé Diet Plan** is designed to work with your lifestyle.
3. Make a commitment: Write down some important reasons for changing your eating habits.
4. Start a food diary and record everything you eat. You can also record your emotions as well.
5. Be consistent and do not give up.
6. Be flexible, if you make a mistake or eat off plan. Then start over the next day with a clean slate.
7. Plan your meals in advance.
8. Congratulate yourself often.

The key to **The Vujá Dé Diet Plan** is Moderation. What is moderation? I am so glad you asked…. It is avoidance of excess by exercising self-control; basically, it's eating only what you need to fuel your body without becoming greedy. Our version of moderation is knowing when to eat and what to eat.

Our program is not designed to starve you; it's designed to give you freedom with a few restrictions like eating five to six small meals each day, spaced apart by about three hours within a certain time frame. And, if the gluttony of food is our weakest link, then we need to check and see what's going on within the soul.

CHAPTER 9

SOUL FOOD

Being side-tracked by doubt creates an open door for your inner critic to control your life. Doubt is simple thoughts that create limitations and insecurities within oneself. When doubt is in control, it has enough power to stop a person right in his or her tracks without them realizing it. For this reason, it is very important to stay ahead of the game when it comes down to doubt, because it does not travel alone. It comes with the immediate family, ancestors, and friends of emotional bondage that feeds on the weaknesses that are buried within the depths of your soul.

Now my question is, "When doubt comes knocking at your door, who is your worst critic?" Could it possibly be you? Maybe or maybe not, but if you leave room for doubt in your life, your inner critic can and will cause you to become envious, insecure, and miserable. However, when you take positive action, it erases doubt; therefore, bringing forth the confidence that will create an atmosphere for you to succeed without being sidetracked. SUCCESS is not based on how much you know—it is based on your determination to learn more than you did the day before and how well you are able to deal with the time that you have available to you.

Once time passes you by—it is gone forever, it cannot be regained. Time management is one of the best-kept secrets of those who are successful; and, it's also one of the biggest obstacles known to man. For that reason, it's time for you to get in on what's working for those who value what they are doing and what they are not doing. Time is a precious gift that's useless if wasted or accident-prone if rushed. We are all guilty of wasting time and rushing, some more than others. However, the individuals who waste a lot of time on a regular basis are usually the ones who tend to complain about NOT having enough time for a healthy lifestyle. In point of fact, time is not usually valued until it runs out.

Effectiveness is the key here. How effective are you with the time that you have available to you? Frankly, it is your effectiveness or ineffectiveness that's going to set the tone for how well you drop the pounds that are keeping you weighted down. For most of us, procrastination is one of our biggest vices; yet, being in a hurry wastes just as much time as procrastination. Regardless of whether a person procrastinates or rush, they both send negative messages of something not being worth their time. Please do not misunderstand me, tight schedules do not make you effective; it makes you exhausted. Balance is the key—it is a balanced schedule that makes you effective; not just at work, but in your personal life as well as with developing and maintaining a healthy lifestyle.

Distractions may come and go; however, when you focus and place value in having a healthy lifestyle, it will maximize your usefulness. And, it may also prevent unnecessary health conditions as well as frustrations or losses later. There will come a time when you may have to limit visitors, limit the time you are on the phone, limit the time you waste chatting, etc. However, everyone has the same amount of time—it's just finding value in the time that you have—hint, hint, this is where discipline comes in. Discipline is the key to managing your time. There is nothing hard about being disciplined; actually, discipline is very easy when you have a plan, but it does require self-control. Nevertheless, it is the lack of planning or the lack of discipline that gets hard and difficult, especially when we are at a loss of what we need to do. Most often, we do not succeed because we are poor managers of our time—poor time managers make excuses. Once time is lost, it can never be regained; and, for that reason, we need to learn how to assume responsibility for it, without allowing our excuses to mask it, or allowing it to become our very own self-imposed burden. Time is on our side, we all have 24 hours a day; so, that means that we are going to have to prioritize our time wisely. First, we need to decide what's important and what's not—doing the important things first, before moving on to the next task. Second, we must learn how to just say, "NO." We do not always have to answer the phone, watch television, listen to the radio, etc.

Anything that is worth having is worth working for! Taking one extra step a day toward your goal will get you to your final destination a whole lot faster with the least amount of effort. It may take a few minutes out of your day; but trust me, one minute will eventually add up to 1 whole hour, and one hour will eventually add up to 24 extra hours toward your goal.

Emotional Tongue

It is imperative that you master your emotional tongue opposed to allowing your emotional tongue to master you. An emotional tongue is basically speaking out of emotion. Yes, it happens to the best of us; and no, this does not apply to the women only. Men are just as emotional as women; they just know how to cover up their emotions a little better than women. This is not a man or woman thing; this is a reality thing of what's mastering you. Emotions that are not dealt with properly could lead to missed opportunities caused by unintentional self-sabotage. How do you prevent this? It's real simple, think before you speak and ask the Holy Spirit to guide your tongue. Sandpaper emotions will always cause people to rub you the wrong way. Regardless of whether you are rubbed the wrong way or not, never make decisions when you are emotionally imbalanced and never manipulate people by becoming too emotional. However, we are all a little rough around the edges in some area of our lives; however, reacting inappropriately will cause us to lose more than we will ever gain. So, watch out for the temper! Giving a person, place, or thing control over our emotions will always keep us in a state of disarray or on an emotional roller-coaster.

It only takes a few seconds to pray before you react. If you don't know what to pray for—just say, "Help me, Lord" or "Holy Spirit, take over." Don't waste your precious time fighting against yourself, the things that cause you pain, or the things that you don't want. Conflict is designed so that you can take the negative energy, and turn it into something positive.

Today, relax and focus on the things that you do want, to ensure that you are able to smooth out those rough edges. Seek peace in all that you do and chaos will find its way out of your life; granting you a double-portion of your blessing for not giving up. From me to you, no matter what's going on in your life, control your emotions to keep the fears of life from sabotaging your inner peace. Trust me, when you can look beyond your bruised ego, you can start breaking down the walls of your hidden fears and limitations. In my opinion, fear represents a lack of faith and insecurities with your capabilities, which are created within oneself.

We all have hidden fears, known and unknown. Fear is created in the mind of an individual and is primarily triggered by esteem battles that appear as fear of failure, fear of being ridiculed, fear of rejection, fear of imperfections, fear of making mistakes, fear of loving again, or fear of success. However, the fear of betrayal could be more devastating than betrayal itself. If you have difficulty trusting someone, your lack of trust could be derived from your childhood. Compounded hurt from people you've allowed yourself to trust will cause you to feel as if everyone has a vendetta against you. Most often, betrayal is a condition that can be reckoned with, if you allow it. More importantly, fear immobilizes your mind and prepares you to create failure by your own actions. In so many words, you set your own self up for failure based on previous experiences or mistakes.

Self-examination is necessary to weed out the superficial attachments to material gain; and, if you want to overcome the fear of failure, you must really find out who you are. For example, you are not your job; you are not the car you drive, you are not money, you are not the clothes you wear, and you are not the neighborhood that you live in. As long as you separate yourself from THINGS—you will not feel the sting of not having them, losing them or the desire to impress others. Secondly, feel the fear of whatever it is, admit to it and set some priorities. Thirdly, keep moving forward, and I promise you that fear will lose its grip on your life. If you don't, the fear of not having enough will keep you wanting more than what you have.

The fear of not having enough will eventually cause you to become greedy and deceitful. Undealt with greed has a way of attracting negative and unproductive people, places, and things in your life; eventually, causing your life to spiral out of control. Always remember, looks are very deceiving—the grass will not always be greener on the other side, especially, when the grass you already have is not properly maintained. As fear begins to release its grip on your life, it's imperative that you become a good steward over what you already have, and stop wasting time on things that are not positive, productive, and fruitful!

Now, after receiving and digesting this Soul Food, **The Vujá Dé Diet Plan** starts with a food diary. Record everything you eat, what you were doing at the time, and how you felt. This tells you about yourself, your temptations, and the emotional states that encourage you to eat or snack. This will indeed pinpoint your emotional triggers that prevent you from losing weight, and it may also help you to lose even more weight once you see how much you are really eating. Here are a few of **The Vujá Dé Diet Plan** tips:

- Instead of eating a piece of candy, simply brush your teeth.

- If you cannot fight off the temptation to cheat, allow yourself one bite and throw the rest away.

- When hunger pains hit you, drink a glass of water, green tea, or juice and wait 10 minutes before eating and see if it passes.

- Set attainable goals. In the beginning, do not set a goal saying "I want to lose 50 pounds." Make it small, saying, "I want to lose 5 pounds a month."

- Get enough sleep, 7-8 hours is enough.

- Try to avoid sugar. Sweet foods invoke the craving for more sugary foods.

- Drink 8 glasses of water a day. Water is a natural diuretic, and it helps to cut down on your water retention. It will also prevent you from overindulging by causing you to feel full, especially when you squeeze a piece of lemon, lime, or orange in your water. Drinking water also wards off infections and diseases by giving your system an adequate flush.

- Diet with a friend or join a support group to keep you motivated.

- Indulge in different activities when the food cravings hit you or when your emotions cause you to want to binge eat. It's best to go to the gym, take a walk, or indulge in a hobby; it will definitely take your mind off eating.

- Do not buy the foods that tempt you; leave it on the shelf at the store.
- If you have a craving for sugar, grab a piece of fruit such as an orange slice, grapes, berries, etc.
- You are only allowed 1 reward night per week.
- You must weigh yourself once a week at the same time.
- Use a saucer to eat meals and leave something on your plate. No "Super-Size" meals period; if you eat out, a kid's meal is ideal.
- Do not shop when you are hungry—eat before you go, period.
- Avoid consuming large quantities of fattening drinks; this includes alcoholic beverages.
- Keep plenty of foods like raw vegetables and popcorn as snacks in between meals.
- Lose weight only for you.
- Chew your food nice and slow, savoring every moment!
- Do not skip meals.
- Exercise 3-4 times a week and make sure you stay hydrated.
- Your goal is to become healthy, NOT THIN! Your body will find its natural set-point, and if your set-point is thin—so be it. If it is not, you must become happy with the frame that God has blessed you with.

- If you find yourself bored, find something to do.

CHAPTER 10

GOOD EATS

Food is designed to fuel us, and anything that God created, He said it was good for us. However, keep in mind with all of the processed food in the market today, we must go back to the simple The Vujá Dé Diet Plan fact-finding question that one must ask: Is it God made or is it Man made? Once we get our attitude in check regarding our life, we are better able to have a better attitude about what we are putting in our bodies.

With **The Vujá Dé Diet Plan,** you are not limited to our food list. However, we do have our foods of **choice**; and, we have a special way of putting the foods together to achieve **The Vujá Dé Diet Plan** results. Nevertheless, you need to learn a little more about the true value of balance first. If you choose to eat whatever you want that's not listed, and you do not get the results that you are looking for, you cannot blame **The Vujá Dé**

Diet Plan—you would have to assume responsibility for that! We believe in discipline, because it does have a domino effect in other areas of our lives as well.

Balancing Act

It is extremely hard to balance our food choices if we are having a hard time balancing our life. However, balance is the key, and the driving force of our passion resides in our ability to dedicate ourselves to that in which is destined to challenge us. What I have definitely found in life is that anything or anyone worth having is worth working for. The dynamics of achieving success in anything or with anyone requires us to persevere through our challenges to achieve a common goal. And, whatever that common goal is—is up to us, and it is our responsibility to work toward it with due diligence.

Do you expect the worst out of life or do you expect the best? How often do we have an expectation about a person, place, or thing and not realize it? Our expectations are based upon our experiences and self-belief. There are some who are fortunate enough to have all good experiences, as there will always be those who have the not so good experiences as well. Fear of failure and the lack of self-confidence are the enemies that impede the development of our positive expectations. If we fail to make the appropriate changes to counteract the effects of our negative expectations, we will soon find that it will become extremely hard to move forward to embrace the opportunities that bring about positive change. When the negative critic from within dominates our thoughts, our expectations in life become very doubtful and insecure.

The power of our expectations are governing factors that contribute to our belief system, therefore creating our known or unknown reality. Our beliefs, desires, and expectations have a way of empowering us or causing us to settle for defeat. However, if we know where we are in our weight loss phase, we are better able to bring a resolve to the issue. Here are few questions to answer before we move to the next phase:

1. Why do you want to lose weight?
2. What's your goal weight?
3. Are you willing to do what it takes to achieve your goal?
4. What's your goal after you lose the weight?
5. How do you plan to keep the weight off?
6. Are you truly losing weight for you, or are you losing weight in order for someone else to accept you?
7. Are you happy with what you look like right now?
8. What are your measurements?

The Vujá Dé Diet Plan
Measurements

Right Arm						
Left Arm						
Chest						
Waist						
Hips						
Right Thigh						
Left Thigh						
Weight						
Date						

Just remember that limitations of our flaws are created in the mind when there is codependency residing in the heart. Everything that we do, say, or react to, contributes to the way in which we deal with ourselves, as well as the way in which we deal with or help others. Challenges will come, and challenges will go; therefore, we must determine what we will hold on to when the challenges leave. Some hold on to resentment, some hold on to anger, some hold on to fear, and some hold on to the ability to let go. And, regardless of what we hold on to, we are held accountable for what we do with and how we react to our experiences. You are here to make a difference! It is through you that a certain amount of people can be reached and it's your responsibility to make a positive impact on them, regardless of your set of challenges.

When dealing with self, it's okay to use our expectations to solve a problem, make a change or empower ourselves because we are not born confident—it is a character trait that is learned. Most often, we will find that confidence is confused with arrogance and vice-versa. Confidence displays the security and strength to take charge, to make changes as well as make effective decisions; whereas, arrogance is the opposite. We will find that arrogant people are really insecure, using the illusion of strength to cover up hidden weaknesses. I feel that whatever we have learned in the past can be unlearned, if we are willing to change our expectations and work through our weaknesses.

As life moves forward for me, when we waste time backtracking, we will soon find ourselves in a competitive race moving three steps forward and two steps back. I am not advocating ignoring the past, because if we do, we are destined to repeat it; however, if the past is all we have to offer, then it's best that we reconsider how we are going to live our future. I have found that holding on to the past will prevent us from living a fulfilled life, and living a fulfilled life will definitely prevent us from indulging in the past. Just take a look around, we will find that the people who are moving in a backward motion are usually the ones that do not have a plan or have a tendency to get stuck in the past. And, rest assured that the ones who are stuck in the past without a plan are also the ones who are resistant to change, regardless of whether it is the right thing to do.

Even if I had to learn a lesson two or three times, I know that God would not place any more on me than I could actually bear. Although I had to streamline my superficial or irrelevant thoughts, I was committed to progression in my life. Despite how it may or may not appear to me, I kept my mind positively focused in the right direction. I also had to realize that everyone may not be going where I am going, they may not look the way I want them to look and they may not have what I expect them to have, but they have a role to play in my life to enable me to become better in all things.

Letting go has been one of the greatest obstacles known to man. Our mind is constantly bombarded with the thoughts of the past, clouding out our dreams, aspirations, and goals. As I see it, if you don't like the way you are living right now, then change the way in which you are living. If you don't like whom you are with right now, find someone that you like. For whatever reason, you feel the way you feel, life is too short to have a bad attitude about the decisions YOU have made to hold on to things that you should have let go of a long time ago.

CHAPTER 11

THE POWER OF VUJÁ DÉ

In order to master **The Vujá Dé Diet Plan**, one must understand the power of setting goals; if not, they will become defeated with this plan. A goal is a road map; it will tell you where you are, what you need to do, and how to get there. What I have found is that those who do not have goals set for themselves, usually wonder aimlessly through life working toward nothing. As a result of working toward nothing, they will soon start settling for things that are not a part of them, not a part of their purpose, and it contradicts everything that they believe in. Consequently, without a goal, plan, or purpose, it will become hard for them to understand and know where they are going.

From this point on, when defining your goal and purpose in life, take whatever time is necessary to study, plan, and think.   This is where **Vujá Dé** comes into effect.....**Vujá Dé** means to change your perception of how you view things; basically, it means in layman's terms, "CHANGE YOUR VIEW."   The way you perceive yourself, the way you perceive life, the value that you place upon yourself, and what you put in your body tells others how you think without you saying one word. Is this real?   Absolutely. Your expressions, your body language, your demeanor, your attitude, or your aura speaks very loud with or without your permission. Now, in order for you to change your perception of how you see yourself, you must design a personal roadmap. Yes, put in writing your step-by-step plan or a list of your ideas on how you intend to use **The Vujá Dé Diet Plan** to accomplish your goals mentally, physically, emotionally, and spiritually.   In this planning process, you must keep each item separate.   Write out your specific goals, purpose, ideas, precepts, or concepts, regardless of how insignificant it may seem to you— write it out.   After each item, write down why you want to achieve it. Here are a few questions to get you started:

1.   What do you value the most?
2.   What is your most important goal?
3.   If you only had 1 year to live, what would you do?
4.   What do you love to do?
5.   What makes you feel important?

6. What's the risk?
7. What are the pros and cons?
8. What are the obstacles involved?
9. What will you have to sacrifice in your life?

In order to commit yourself to your goal, you must enter into a binding contract. This will become your contract between you and God. When you continuously embed this burning desire on your subconscious mind, it will become a desire that will consume you until you have achieved it. Try to be as clear and detailed as you can. Include all of the goals you want to achieve, the knowledge you will need, what occupation you want to engage in, the kind of person you want to become, the income you want to earn, etc. Aim for the gift that is within you; if you do not—you will miss out every time.

There are times when you may have to keep your goals to yourself, so that you will not put yourself in a position to be talked about, criticized, or discouraged from achieving your goals. I have found that setting goals:

- Helps you to stay focused and achieve more.
- Prevents confusion from within.
- Provides more confidence.
- Gives you a peace of mind.
- Creates more joy and satisfaction.

- Keeps you motivated to perform at your best.

Get rid of the shoulda, coulda, and woulda syndrome and use "I can, I will, and I expect." Your goals in life will become your treasure map to success. It may not be easy, because if it were easy, everyone would be able to do it. God will not place a desire in your heart that He cannot manifest. After you have signed your commitment, read it aloud at least 7 times each morning and 7 times before going to bed at night for 40 days and once thereafter until your goal is achieved. This will help you get focused on doing what you have to do, to get to where you need to be in life. In order to eliminate backtracking, you must have your road map handy at all times, so that you can make the right turn at the right time. In my opinion, it is best to mark your destination on your roadmap, and ask God to allow the Holy Spirit to become your tour guide to accomplish your goal.

In creating a plan for succeeding with your goals in life, you need to know what it is that you want to believe in. That is why it is very important to plan your success and make it happen by asking yourself 7 integrity finding questions:

1. Can I honestly ask God's help in striving to reach this goal?
2. Will it get me where I want to go?

3. Will it violate God's laws?

4. Will it violate my conscience or override my purpose?

5. Will it violate the rights of others?

6. Will my family be able to enjoy the rewards of my accomplishments?

7. Am I willing to do what it takes in order to succeed?

It is possible that you may have to revise your goal list on a certain day every month. Put the achieve goals on your "Thank God Victory List." And, put your major goals on a 3 x 5 card and carry it everywhere you go. When you have to make a big decision, ask yourself:

1. Is it according to the will of God?

2. Will it get me closer to my goal or purpose?

3. Will it help me or hinder me?

4. How do I feel about it? If you feel confused, disoriented, or have any type of funny feeling, this should be a red flag.

A strong enough passion for something will enhance our sense of direction that will drive us to our goal or away from our goal. Just remember, our sense of direction is often blinded by our inability to recognize our goal setting capabilities. For example, we achieve many goals on a daily basis; such as getting up in the morning, taking care of ourselves, taking care of our family, cooking a meal, driving to our destination, getting to work on time, etc. Yet, we consider ourselves a failure when we do not achieve a goal that has our attention. All goals, big or small, deserve our attention! Think through your goals and do not set them too low, but you also want your goal attainable, and become thankful for the small goals on a daily basis, and those big goals will come.

When you know your strengths, weaknesses, skills, values, attitudes, and interests, you will become better prepared for the surprises that life may spring up on you. In this program we have 10 Principles regarding **The Power of Vujá Dé**; and, it will be your responsibility to work on these Principles until you have mastered them.

1. **Continue to Learn**. Learning is the key ingredient in any form of success. You are responsible for improving and increasing your learning capacity. When you become committed to learning and polishing up your skills in the spirit of excellence, success will come knocking at your door. Regardless of what you do or do not do in life, never stop learning.

2. **Believe in Yourself**. Confidence will supersede low self-esteem any day. Most failures in life are derived from giving up too soon; not only that,

giving up on ourselves has contributed to the distorted outlook we may have about ourselves. Despite what you may or may not have to give up, never give up on you.

3. **Free Your Mind to Think**. You must be able to think inside the box, outside the box, around the box, and through the box.   Even though you want to keep your mind free to think, you must also guard your mind against any unwanted negative thoughts.   Just remember, all of our successes and failures in life start in the mind. For that reason, you are free to create the life you desire based on the thoughts that you think and the actions you take when thinking inside, outside, around, and through the box of life.

4. **Be Open and Honest**. Deception crushes more relationships than we care to imagine. You will find when you are trustworthy; people will trust your actions, reactions, and decisions.   Your honesty and integrity will take you further than having a hidden agenda of deception.   Just remember that trust is not always given, it is earned by the way in which you carry yourself and your ability to be straightforward about your intent or motive.

5. **You must be willing to step outside your comfort zone**. You must be willing to do what others are afraid to do. Taking a risk is risky business; however, without a risk, nothing is gained. When we are willing to take a risk, it will determine the level in which we achieve our desired goals. It is through our ability to move outside of our comfort zone that governs our ability to venture out into the great unknown.

6. **Exercise Self-Control**. We must set a guard over our actions, reactions, and thoughts to ensure that we maintain control over self. We are designed to control self, and if we don't, then we cannot expect anyone to do it for us. When we are out of control, rest assured that other areas of our lives will spiral out of control as well. Having control over self, does not make us a control freak, unless we violate the will of others or force others to make decisions based upon our expectations. Therefore, you must become a good steward over self or a good manager over self, and you will find that you are better able to master your ability to communicate with others without becoming too emotional.

7. **Assume Responsibility**. We must learn how to take responsibility for our actions, reactions, our attitude, and our mishaps in life. Of course, we

are all subject to error; however, it is imperative that we learn from our mistakes to prevent a life of déjà vu. An unlearned or ignored lesson is destined to repeat itself in our life with a greater impact. Even though it is easier to pass the blame; but, we do not have time to pass the blame. Today, assume responsibility and all of your mishaps in life will become stepping stones of opportunity.

8. **You must become disciplined**. Without discipline, we have disorder or compounded confusion. When we lack discipline, we will lack positive or productive results in our lives. Without discipline, we have a tendency to become lazy—when we become lazy about accomplishing the desires of our heart, we tend to expect others to do that in which we are not willing to do for ourselves. If you want to achieve greatness, slothfulness is not going to get it! Get up, develop a plan of action and get moving; because, if you are going to succeed, your commitment to yourself is required.

9. **Commit to a Plan with added flexibility**. When we commit to a goal or a plan, we must keep an open mind. There are times when we may have to adjust our goals or plans, so we must remain open to change. A closed minded

individual will find that he or she is inflexible to change, regardless of whether it's positive or negative. Our commitments in life require flexibility because people, places, things, and needs change.

10. **You must be willing to share.** The Law of Reciprocity (to give and to receive) is the door to true prosperity. Be Generous. We are just as responsible for giving as we are for receiving. You must be able to give, without giving in to becoming a miser. This is definitely what seed, time, and harvest are all about. Lastly, what you make happen for others, God can and will make happen for you, guaranteed!

Once the attitude adjustment has been made, then you are ready to begin **The Vujá Dé Diet Plan**. So, let's begin our journey to finding Y.O.U.

CHAPTER 12

TIMING IS EVERYTHING

We cannot save everyone, but it's our responsibility to do our part in making a true difference. Throughout my journey in life, I have found that communication is one of our most invaluable commodities. If we have a desire to be understood, we must first understand through effective listening. When we do not listen, we will find that we tend to miss out on the essence of what true living is all about.

When we are at the crossroads of survival, the thoughts that we think determines the real essence of who we are, what we will become, what or whom we attract, and which direction we take. One of the biggest issues that we all face is to figure out what to do with our lives. Nevertheless, in the figuring process, we often get our insurance policies together preparing for death, forgetting about preparing to live. Living our lives to the fullest is often overlooked because we become so busy going from here to there—not realizing that there is more to life than our present situation.

Our enemies will become our footstool of greatness if we allow him or her to play his or her role in our lives without becoming bitter about the circumstances or situation that's presented to us. It's through our enemies that we will find our nuggets of wisdom and understanding, if we do not become too emotional. Our emotions inhibit our ability to grab the source of wisdom needed to make all of our enemies become the footstool that's propelling us to the next level; therefore, it's imperative that we allow our enemies to make us better and not bitter. When we are bitter, we actually prevent wisdom from attaching itself to us; as a matter of fact, bitterness opens the door to jealousy and envy, to further break down the emotional bond; therefore, breaking down the relationship.

It does not matter what people think or say about you that matters, it's what you are saying about you that really makes the difference. So what if people throw dirt at you or on you—just step up to the next level with your head up high as you learn how to develop the voice from within, the counselor of your higher self. My friend, God has given you the Holy Spirit as your counselor; why not allow Him to work for you and through you to accomplish your goals and achieve your desired weight loss through **The Vujá Dé Diet Plan**.

Our Program is very symbolic due to the fact that Man was created in the Bible on the 6th day. Although, most do not recognize the number 6 as being symbolic; however, **The Vujá Dé Diet Plan** is going to reveal how symbolic the number is, and how it can help us take charge over our lives. The next reason for 6 being symbolic for us is that God took 6 days to create everything, and took the 7th day to rest; therefore, letting us know how important it is to rest our bodies at least one day out of the week.

On this program, we follow the same principle—we use the structured plan for 6 days, and on the 7th day, we must rest our bodies; therefore, creating a free day to eat whatever we so desire. Furthermore, as a part of our structure, timing is everything. We have an eating schedule that will allow us to only consume certain types of food based on the widely used time clock.

To make it very simple, if we look at the clock closely, in the morning the hour short hand is going up, and in the afternoon, the hour short hand is going down in 6-hour increments. Therefore, in the morning we want to raise our level of spirituality symbolically in that 6-hour increment from 6 a.m. – 11:59 a.m. and 6:01 p.m. – 11:59 p.m. We can only partake of foods that will increase our level of consciousness when the short arrow on the clock is rising. Now, 12:00 p.m. – 6:00 p.m., we will find that the short hand arrow goes downward, and our ultimate goal is to lose weight. Therefore, symbolically we can only eat regular foods during this time to ensure that we are mentally lining up our bodies to lose weight, or better yet, allowing the pounds to fall off. And, from 12:00 a.m. – 5:59 a.m. is mandatory rest.

The Clock Short
Rising

The Clock Short Hand
Falling

Once you become accustomed to eating in such a manner, you will soon find that there's more to life than just existing here on earth.

CHAPTER 13

THE VUJÁ DÉ MEAL PLAN

Once that part of your life comes together, it is only fair to show you how **The Vujá Dé Diet Plan** will fit into your daily life. If you have Dietary Supplements, take them 30 minutes prior to your meal. You can also start your day with **The Vujá Dé Diet Plan Tonic which is available online at:**

www.RubyFleurcius.com

We keep our meal plan very simple, choose 1 Fruit and 1 Food Item from the **Vujá Dé Food List**, or choose 1 Fruit and 1 **Vujá Dé** Super Food mixed into a smoothie for breakfast. Then, for your morning snack, choose 1 Fruit and 1 Dairy Item from the **Vujá Dé Food List.**

The Vujá Dé Diet Plan

Breakfast List
6:00 a.m. – 11:59 a.m.

Choose One Item

Apples, Grapefruit, Lime,
Cranberries, Lemon, Mango,
Orange, Papaya, Peaches,
Pineapples, Coconut, or Pomegranate

Choose One Item

Oatmeal, Cream of Wheat, or Grits

The Vujá Dé Diet Plan

Snack List
6:00 a.m. – 11:59 a.m.

Choose One Item

Apples, Grapefruit, Lime,
Cranberries, Lemon, Mango,
Orange, Papaya, Peaches,
Pineapples, Coconut, or Pomegranate

Choose One Dairy Item

Skim Milk, Soy Milk, Almond Milk,
Cottage Cheese, Cheese, or Yogurt

If you get hungry before lunch or dinner, simply have Jell-O or eat an extra apple.

For Lunch and Dinner

All portions must fit in your saucer plate; therefore, you must leave room for your veggies and grains that can only be consumed between the hours of 12:00 p.m. and 6 p.m. **The Vujá Dé Diet Plan** suggested time for eating is 1 meal at 12:00 p.m. and 1 meal at 5:00 p.m. However, the choice is yours regarding what time you will eat between the hours of 12:00 p.m. and 6 p.m. You can have:

1 Protein, 1 Starch, 2 Vegetables, and 1 Fat for each meal.

During these 2 structured meals, **The Vujá Dé Diet Plan** does not allow the consumption of fruits or desserts while having your meal. However, you are able to have certain fruits as a snack in between your meals during the hours of 12:00 p.m. and 6 p.m. This plan is not designed to deprive you; it is designed to bring balance to your body, while provoking your body to burn the unwanted fat that's needed to get your body to its natural set-point.

The Vujá Dé Diet Plan

Regular Food Choices
12:00 p.m. – 6:00 p.m.

Choose 1 Protein for Lunch and Dinner

Beans, Chicken, Seafood,
Eggs, Fish, Turkey,
Tofu, Nuts, or Peanut Butter

Choose 1 Starch(Grain) for Lunch and Dinner

Corn, White Potatoes, Yams,
Oatmeal, Cream of Wheat, Sweet Potatoes,
Pasta, Bread, or Rice

Choose 2 Vegetables for Lunch and Dinner

Asparagus, Bean sprouts, Broccoli, Cabbage, Greens,
carrots, Cauliflower, Celery, Cucumber, Eggplant,
Onions, Kale, Lettuce, Spinach, Green
Peppers, Radishes, Rhubarb, Squash, String Beans,
Tomato, Turnips, Zucchini, Hot Peppers, Garlic, Beets
Mushrooms, or Ginger

The Vujá Dé Diet Plan

Regular Food Choices
12:00 p.m. – 6:00 p.m.

Choose 1 Fat for Lunch and Dinner

Light Butter, Light Mayonnaise, Corn Oil,
Olive Oil, Coconut Oil, or Nut Oil

1 Tablespoon Allowed Per Meal

After 6:01 p.m. you are allowed 1 fruit, plenty of water and green tea for the rest of the evening until 11:59 p.m. If you get hungry during the night, grab some Jell-O to avoid any self-sabotage. However, after Midnight, you can have absolutely nothing but water until 6:00 a.m.

The Vujá Dé Diet Plan

Regular Food Snack Choices
12:00 p.m. – 6:00 p.m.

Choose 1 Fruit In Between Lunch and Dinner

Apples, Grapefruit, Blue Berries, Bananas, Cantaloupe, Honeydew,Cranberries, Lemon, Mango, Orange, Papaya, Peaches, Pineapples, Strawberries, Raspberries,Watermelon, Pear, Grapes, Plums, Pomegranate, Cherries, Nectarines, Lime, Avocado, Coconut, Fruit cup, or Fruit Smoothie

The Vujá Dé Diet Plan

Choose One Item

Apples, Grapefruit, Lime,
Cranberries, Lemon, Mango,
Orange, Papaya, Peaches,
Pineapples, Coconut, or Pomegranate

This weight management plan works, and if you dedicate yourself to this plan, your body will plateau at its set-point with the results that you will be pleased with. Guaranteed!

CHAPTER 14

THE CRUTCH

We need people, and people need us. I know that there is a lot of hype about being independent; and, yes, we all should be independent assuming responsibility for our own lives. However, we must also have an openness to interdependence as well. Interdependence is our ability to work together with people to accomplish a common goal in the "WE" form—in so many words, "Teamwork." In order to stay on point with this plan, it is possible that we may have to recruit someone to encourage us through the process. It is imperative to get our bodies up and moving—we need exercise and exercise need us. Don't think about exercise being repulsive, just keep it simple and fun. Do 10 minutes in the morning, 10 minutes in the afternoon, and 10 minutes in the evening. That is an easy 30 minutes of moving, and it's even easier if we are connected to others. We need to supercharge our metabolism, and if we do not, it will naturally slow down on us. We do not have to run a marathon, but our blood needs to stay warm in order to flow through our veins properly.

It is not just about burning calories as most would think, it is about your body pumping blood through your arteries properly without developing clots. Think about this, when you sit there doing nothing your blood sits there too, getting cold in the air conditioning, doing nothing! Your body has to do all the work, and you are not helping it out any—the body's natural response is to slow down; therefore; collecting clots, cholesterol, stored fat, sicknesses, viruses, etc.; therefore; weakening our immune system. The more your metabolism slows down, the more emotional and mental imbalance you will become as well! However, if you are boosting your metabolism, it does not have the time to think about what it's going to collect; it will burn it as long as you are not overloading it with the wrong foods, toxins, or drugs!

We cannot sabotage ourselves by not moving our bodies, and the good news is that there are so many ways to do it. Always eat in moderation, never overdo it! Discipline is key, and if your craving cannot wait until your free day, then you can rest assured that it is emotional eating, so get a grip.

Our interconnectedness and interdependence with others is a great way to achieve that in which we cannot do for ourselves. There are times when greater success can be attained through a combined effort of those who are able to accentuate the greatness that's already within us, without us becoming dependent upon them. Of course, trust must be developed in some way; however, it should never prevent us from becoming a team player in all that we do, say, or think. In order to maximize our interdependency, we must hone into our ability to become a motivator or motivatee. As we all know, motivation is the key factor in communicating effectively with self, others, and our environment.

Our environment has a paramount effect on us whether we admit it or not. And, if our environment is comprised of selfishness—we have a tendency to become selfish as well, if we do not take the initiative to make the necessary changes. When we become willing to exhaust all of our resources, we therefore put ourselves in a position to overcome any known or unknown adversity that prevents us from taking responsibility for ourselves. Therefore, giving us the ability to achieve the desires of our heart or giving us the courage to get rid of what's not working in our environment. We are the paradigm of our environment, we are the paradigm of our belief system, we are the paradigm of our thoughts, we are the paradigm of our actions, and we are the paradigm of our attitude. If we want our paradigm to change, we must change or adjust our level of dependency, as well as our mindset.

It is through your mindset that governs your beliefs, and it is through your beliefs that govern the perception you have over your reality or the perspective that you have about yourself. My friend, it's imperative that you avail yourself to become interconnected with your environment; therefore, enabling you to better understand whether the people, places, and things in your life are enhancing or limiting your full potential.

CHAPTER 15

THE ENCOURAGER

We are in a love famine more now than ever in history—we don't know who to love, how to love, where to love, and when to love. It seems as if love has become a mystery to all who seek it. Real love is loving God first as you are a spiritual being, then truly loving yourself from the inside out, while allowing the love that you have for both to extend outwardly to others; therefore, creating sound relationships that are able to withstand the ups and downs of life until you find what you are looking for in life. Here is what L.O.V.E. means to me:

Let go - Release attachments.
Overcome - Rejections
Validate - Speak positive, instead of negative thinking.

Empower - Help build up people without tearing them down.

If you can find a way to Let go, Overcome, Validate, and Empower, you will find a hidden strength from within that will trump any form of defeat. Guaranteed!

The greatest encourager known to man is the encourager that resides within oneself. Even if people cannot see what we see, we still have to encourage ourselves, even if people do not believe in our dreams, we still have to encourage ourselves, even when people laugh at our dreams, we still have to believe in ourselves; and, it does not matter who believes in what we believe in, as long as we believe in ourselves. We are our best cheerleader, and we can also become our worst critic, especially when we cannot get what we want; and, whichever one we choose, our life will become a direct reflection of that particular choice. There are times when we become so caught up in the busyness of life that we do not take the time to encourage ourselves; therefore, we look for and expect others to do what we have not taken the time to do for ourselves.

You can be whatever you desire as long as you do not give up on your greatest supporter and that is YOU. Don't forget, after you encourage yourself, make sure you encourage someone else to activate the Law of Reciprocity. Listed below are the must-know principles of this program:

1. Know that you must give each day back to God.
2. Know that you must pray and place God first in your life.
3. Know that you must prioritize God, self, spouse, children, and then others as a part of the Divine Order.
4. Know that no one can take your power from you unless you choose to give it away.
5. Know that happiness is a choice that you choose on a moment-by-moment basis.
6. Know that you are a gift from God, and resentment cannot steal your blessings from you, unless you give in to it.
7. Know that FEAR cannot stop the blessings God has for you. Always know that your blessing is on the other side of what you fear—Push through it!
8. Know that your gift will make room for you, and it will set you before men in high places.
9. Know that you are blessed to do what you do, and guilt has no place in your life.
10. Know that favor will open doors of opportunity for you.
11. Know that you must be willing to make the necessary sacrifices.
12. Know that a good name is chosen, and you must lead by example.
13. Know that you must accept responsibility for your actions and reactions.

14. Know that God can equip you, use you, and teach you what you need to know.
15. Know that risks are necessary for the challenges that will come your way.
16. Know that fault-finding is not conducive to where you are going in life.
17. Know that you must share and take action when necessary.
18. Know that communication is mandatory to achieve the desires of your heart
19. Know that you do not have to entertain negative people, places, and things.
20. Know that mistakes and failures are just stepping stones designed to get you to the next level.
21. Know that you must encourage, inspire, and motivate others regardless of what you are going through.
22. Know that you must be willing to celebrate what God has done for you and through you to show your appreciation for His divine grace and mercy.
23. Know the value of seed, time, and harvest.
24. Know that you must be willing to love and serve others.
25. Know the Law of Reciprocity as well as the Law of Cause and Effect.
26. Know that God has your back when nobody else will.
27. Know that you must complete the exercises in this Plan.

28. Know that you must follow-through to develop discipline.
29. Know that you have the POWER to change your thoughts at any given time.
30. Know that you have the choice to expel negativity out of your life.
31. Know that you cannot blame others for your situation, actions, or experiences.
32. Know that God loves a cheerful, humble, and faithful servant.
33. Know that wisdom requires you to think before you speak.
34. Know that kind words will turn away wrath, allowing you to get your point across.
35. Know that when you communicate, you must look into the eyes of the person that you are speaking to.
36. Know that you should never give your power away by not assuming responsibility for your actions, reactions, thoughts, and conversations.
37. Know that every lesson in life is WISDOM for you to share.
38. Know that your past has no power over you if you use it as a TOOL to build your life or the lives of others.
39. Know that you are good enough for the gift that God has placed inside of you. You are the Best Y.O.U. that you have.

40. Know that you must be quick to forgive and move on to free your mind of unwanted clutter.

41. Know that you do not have to tolerate poor behavior, excuse yourself nicely.

42. Know that confrontation is not necessary when it's so easy to walk away as the bigger person.

43. Know that if anger is sparked in a conversation, you must become silent until a level of peace is established; if not, excuse yourself.

44. Know that your character is on the line every time you open your mouth.

45. Know that your reputation is your lifeline, it's not what people think about you—it's what you think about you that counts! Hold fast to your integrity.

46. Know that when your conscience becomes your guide, you are able to truly live in peace with yourself.

47. Know that the past cannot hold you back if you release it.

48. Know that forgiveness is the TRUMP CARD you pull when you have gotten a bad deal; therefore, giving you the grace and mercy to heal, letting go without hating!

49. Know that you can overcome any obstacle because God will not place more on you than you can tolerate.

50. Know that you have the ability to create a win-win situation out of anything.

51. Know that you are here to inspire others.

52. Know that you must positively affirm everyone, even if you are smarter or wiser than they are—you must always appear humble. Arrogance is a forbidden character trait for where you are going!

53. Know that you treat your enemies with kindness even when they betray you. Just keep your distance with a smile on your face and love them anyway.

54. Know that it is better to say less and do more.

55. Know that you must live every day like it is your last day, taking nothing for granted.

56. Know that you must smile even when you don't have anything to smile about—it is medicine for the soul.

57. Know that you must focus on your goals in life and not your obstacles.

58. Know that you must look for the good in all things, even when it does not appear to be there.

59. Know that you must leave no stone unturned. You must exhaust all of your resources.

60. Know that you cannot allow anyone to push your emotional trigger buttons unless they are positive.

61. Know that you must always expect the unexpected, so that you are never disappointed. Life happens, and you can always keep a smile on your face if you remove the expectations off of people, and place them on yourself. However, you would never tell them of course!

62. Know that you are a GENIUS at something, and it is up to you to find out what it is.
63. Know that you must learn how to let go and not stress out.
64. Know that you cannot solve every problem; you can only do your part.
65. Know that you have to relax and not respond to everything.
66. Know that you cannot overthink issues.
67. Know that procrastination is disguised as the fear of failure or confusion that needs to be dealt with immediately.
68. Know that you have a choice of which direction you take in life.
69. Know that when you determine your values and standards, it is much easier to determine your purpose.
70. Know that you cannot wander aimlessly expecting to achieve greatness.
71. Know that complaining is not an attribute that's conducive to positive living.
72. Know that when you judge others out of jealousy or envy, you bring judgment back to your own house; therefore, speak the truth in love.
73. Know that when you have your plan in writing, it seals the deal with the Universe.
74. Know that life becomes easier when you know what you want, when you have it in writing, when

you have it in your heart, and when you do not deviate from the plan.

75. Know that you have to pay attention to what life is trying to say to you.

76. Know that you must learn something new every day to keep your mind fresh.

77. Know that it is always good to lend a helping hand, expecting nothing in return.

78. Know that it is always good to respect your elders.

79. Know that the best leaders are the best followers and vice-versa.

80. Know that you must be on your best behavior at all times.

81. Know that it is best to always wish people well.

82. Know that you must be grateful for all things.

83. Know that you cannot be afraid to say what's on your mind or ask for what you want.

84. Know that whatever you desire, pay it forward to activate the Law of Reciprocity.

85. Know that you must give your mind time to think in total silence.

86. Know that you say "please" and "thank-you" to people.

87. Know that you must be prompt; it is not good to be late.

88. Know that there is no need to be rude to anyone.

89. Know that you must exercise self-respect in every area of your life.

90. Know that you must venture out of your comfort zone.
91. Know that you must multi-task in order to get things accomplished from time-to-time.
92. Know that you may have to think outside, inside, around, and through the box in order to get what you want.
93. Know that you have to follow your instincts.
94. Know that you cannot make excuses for your mishaps in life.
95. Know that you must remain true to thyself.
96. Know that your little becomes much when you appreciate it and place it in the Hands of the Lord.
97. Know that with every "no" you are that much closer to a "yes."
98. Know that you will have better results in life when you pray about permanent decisions before you make them.
99. Know that if you need a little courage on your journey, simply take a big **ROAR!** Trust me, it works.

CHAPTER 16

NATURAL SECRETS

Your metamorphic stage of life is basically preparing you to be a success from the inside out. Of course, everyone will go through this phase in their lives; some will survive after the change and some will not. Whatever is going on from within will determine your outer world and the people, places, and things that you attract in it. However, being a success from the inside out is much easier than being a success from the outside in. Building substance from within will help you deal with the outside reality on a daily basis. Even so, it is very important that you strive every day not to become a byproduct of the negative side of your past. You are the only one that can determine what success is for you. So, break out of your little cocoon and release the hidden treasures that are inside of you. No more shoulda, coulda, and woulda—Just do it. Yes, it may get a little uncomfortable, but true achievement comes about when you step outside of your comfort zone into the unknown, leaving a legacy worth talking about.

The Trump Card

The true power of who we are is wrapped up in our ability to pray. Prayer has been the most powerful key to my survival, not just in the bad times or moments of desperation, but in the good times as well. It has been a great tool that has changed my life tremendously. I thank God for the power of prayer and my ability to share this information with you.

Prayer is the communication of a sincere, humble request to God. Praying intensifies your ability to face life, make the right decisions, and have the spiritual growth to keep you on a straight and narrow path in seeking His righteousness. Prayer gives you access to the gifts of His divine answers, and is also the key to your blessings and freedom from bondage. This is the power that lies dormant within you that is an essential ingredient in building a relationship with God. Prayer becomes powerful only when it is used in conjunction with faith. "Whatever things you ask when you pray, believe that you receive them, and you will have them," (Mark 11:24, NKJV).

It also helps you to stay focused on your spiritual well-being, and it will also give you the ability to claim the promises of God in the midst of spiritual attacks and adversity. Praying gives you the ability to confess your thoughts, troubles, weaknesses, sins, strengths, desires, thanksgivings, faithfulness, and dependency on someone other than self. You do not have to go to college, acquire a special skill or a license to attain dynamic praying abilities. They will come naturally with practice. It's very simple—pray and ask God for what you need, pray for others, and thank Him. If you don't know how to pray, ask God to teach you; if you do not have wisdom, courage, or strength, ask for it! You may say at times, "God knows what I need," and you are right—He does know what you need before you ask, but He wants you to know and understand what you need as well. Just keep on asking, and you will be given what you ask for. Keep on looking, and you will find. Keep on knocking, and the door will be opened.

God is bigger than any problem you are facing. Don't be afraid to go to Him, for He knows all and He will guide you. If there is a situation with you, in your relationships, with your children, or on your job, whatever it may be, place it in His hands and leave it there. There is no need for complaints if you put Him in control. Just give thanks and consider it done. This is where your faith comes in; if you find yourself continuing to complain about the situation that is an indication that you have not placed it in God's hands, and you have lost your faith in Him. Listed below are a few tips on prayer:

In prayer you must **NEVER**:

1. Pray to harm someone.
2. Pray for evil against someone.
3. Pray for the death of someone.
4. Pray for total control over someone.
5. Pray for another person's possessions.   That means coveting!
6. Pray to force someone to love you or fall in love with you.
7. Pray to break up someone's home.
8. Pray to show off your talents to boost your own ego.
9. Pray out of selfishness, pride, or greed.
10. Pray for someone to do anything against his or her will.

All of these are negative prayers! If you send out negative prayers, you will reap negativity. God has created everyone with a will of his or her own; do not attempt to violate another person's ability or will to choose when you are praying. Always pray for God's assistance in helping that individual with whatever the problem is. Here are a few tips on prayer:

Positive Prayer consists of:

1. Addressing the prayer with praise to God.

2. Asking for God's will to be done in all aspects of your life.
3. Requesting your provisioning or needs for that day, such as food, strength, wisdom, petition, supplication, and intercession.
4. Confession of sins, known and unknown.
5. Protection and deliverance from all temptations.
6. Thanksgiving. Give thanks for all things.

Prayer helps us fine-tune our developmental process to enable us to view people, places, and things differently while enhancing our personal excellence. As we very well know, growing is a natural part of life; and, it definitely takes time to develop an understanding of our own process of achievement. Just because we make an achievement in a certain area of our lives, does not necessarily mean that we are able to excel in that particular area automatically without communicating with God. For example, we have a couple that finally committed to each other to get married; however, just because they decided to get married, does not necessarily make him or her a good wife or husband, nor does it make them soul mates—they are a work in progress and so are you. Our expectations, as well as our attitude, are key players in how we bring forth a mirror image of what we desire.

Embracing the humbling experience to get on your knees will help strengthen your backbone so that you can stand up straight. Having a weak backbone does not always mean that you are a weak person, it just means that you will fall quickly—whether it is falling by the wayside, falling mentally/emotionally or falling in your faith, it's a fall indeed. A weak backbone creates a sense of desperation: desperate for love, desperate for a friend, desperate to be seen, desperate for control, desperate for attention, desperate to be at the top, desperate, desperate, desperate, and the list goes on. Furthermore, a desperate spirit does not attract quality people; it attracts those who feed off of desperate people. BEWARE!!! There is nothing wrong with humbling yourself with a little prayer. Humility is the true sign of controllable strength; as a matter of fact, it is the main ingredient that prevents you from becoming snobbish, rude, arrogant, selfish, inconsiderate, or disrespectful.

The 2nd Trump Card

Meditation is one vital ingredient in life that most of us are missing. Actually, prayer is our way of talking to God and meditation is our way of listening to God as we review, purge, and manifest what we want and do not want in our lives.

Often enough, the thought of sitting still creates more unrest than the process of meditation itself. Meditation is a process of thinking, pondering, and releasing. This process gives us the ability to think through what we are doing, why we are doing, how we are doing, when we are doing, and where we are doing. Meditation allows our inner man to speak, giving us the ability to understand our true greatness and the unlimited potential that we possess from within. Can you succeed without meditating? Absolutely, we can succeed without meditating; but, we must take into account whether or not it is going to last. When our outer man wants to dominate, we must determine whether our success is going to last, whether our peace is going to last, whether our mental stability is going to last, etc. The stress of it all, will cause the best of us to create self-sabotage or to create booby-traps in other areas of our lives; and most often, it shows up in our bodies.

Although, there are many different forms of meditation; however, I want you to develop your own form of meditation that works just for you. Now, in order to truly master a particular area of your life, you will need to master the ability to follow the inner guide from within through the process of meditation, but not limited to meditation only. The empire that you truly desire from within, must be built in your mind before it makes its way to reality. Everything you have, do, or become will be formed as a thought first.

I have found that spring cleaning from within is an excellent way of getting rid of the cobwebs that block your vision daily or the cobwebs that may have blocked your vision over a period of time. As a matter of fact, when the battles are raging from within, a soulful cleaning from within will create a harmony that keeps you balanced temporarily. Although a soulful cleansing is only temporary, it is extremely effective if you are consistent. A soulful cleaning consists of getting rid of negative thoughts, actions, and reactions through prayer, fasting, and meditation. The process of prayer and meditation does not take a lot of skill or talent; it starts with a DECISION—a decision to change our negative patterns into positive ones. It's imperative that you find a way to clean up the dust that may have settled in your thoughts, actions, or reactions. By doing so, this will ensure that you do not get build-up in other areas of your life, preventing you from becoming more than what you are right now.

Peace and calmness contribute to our effectiveness. Change is in your hands, a new outlook is in your hands, wholeness and harmony are in your hands. Why not use the tools that you have to get what you want, positively! All that's required is for you to pay attention to the inner voice or inner feelings that God has divinely placed within you. Here are a few tips on meditating:

1. Determine the location in which you feel comfortable meditating.
2. Decide what time you are going to meditate daily.
3. Decide how long you are going to meditate.
4. Meditate every day.
5. Always sit in an upright position to prevent yourself from falling asleep.

6. Slowly take deep and long breaths, filling your lungs, and then exhaling.
7. This is your personal private time with yourself; make sure you are not disturbed.
8. You can meditate on a Biblical passage or over an issue.
9. Do not over analyze or complicate your meditation. Just keep it simple.
10. Keep an open mind and let go of everything.
11. Allow yourself to become relaxed.

Simply, tell each individual part of your body to relax. Relax your breathing. Relax your mind. Relax your muscles from head to toe. Allow all the pressures of life to be released through the soles of your feet. Every time you breathe in, imagine releasing the stresses and pressures of life when you exhale as you surrender your body to the greatness from within.

The 3rd Trump Card

You are like a sponge, soaking up everything around you, positively or negatively. If you want to feel better, look better, think better, or treat yourself/others better—GO EXERCISE; especially, when you feel a stress attack coming to invade your sanity. Most people use exercise to lose weight; as of today, you will now use exercise to lose stress. Get creative with your exercising; it does not have to be boring; frankly, walking is one of the best forms of exercise, so why not combine that with prayer, and call it walking meditation as you grow toward your greatness.

Personal growth compiled with spiritual growth gives you the option, as well as the opportunity to excel in everything that you do. It's amazing that when you believe that you have something valuable to offer others, the "HOW TO" develops! Just remember that God will meet you at the level of your expectation; especially when you are willing and dedicated to work together with others to produce something positive. Today, make the turn-around to embrace true greatness while others talk, yearn, and waste time.

In conclusion, we are able to overcome or work through any type of obstacles if we learn how to become humble enough to set goals, work on them, believe in ourselves, pray, fast, and meditate. Of course, distractions will come because they are designed to impede upon our goals to keep us distracted, cause us to fail, or to cause us to start making excuses for not succeeding. On this journey, I have found that there are 3 types of people:

1. People who wish things could happen.
2. People who stand around to talk about & criticize what happens.
3. People that have the faith to make things happen and to become effective.

When you have a plan or road map to follow, no matter what happens in your life, you can always get back on track, no matter what! Therefore, write the vision, make it plain, and your healthy lifestyle will begin to serve you very, very well. Guaranteed!

Congratulations! You are done. You have completed **The Vujá Dé Diet Plan**. Now, go out, take everything that you have learned and put your plan to work. Be Blessed and Be a Blessing to Someone Else.

Ruby Fleurcius

www.ingramcontent.com/pod-product-compliance
Lightning Source LLC
LaVergne TN
LVHW021458080426
835509LV00018B/2331